ALCHEMY
The Soul of Astrology

Clare Martin

The Wessex Astrologer

Published in 2020 by
The Wessex Astrologer Ltd
PO Box 9307
Swanage
BH19 9BF

For a full list of our titles go to www.wessexastrologer.com

Cover design by Jonathan Taylor

A catalogue record for this book is available at The British Library

ISBN 9781910531396

Contents

Heaven above
Heaven below
Stars above
Stars below
All that is above
Also is below
Grasp this
And rejoice

Kircher, "Oedipus Aegyptiacus", II, Class X, Ch. V, p.414.

List of Illustrations

Illustrations

	in *Clavis*: Journal of Occult Arts, Letters and Experience Volume 3: Cipher and Stone.
Figure 25:	Sun and Moon dragons, from *Theatrum Chemicum Britannicum* (1652), Elias Ashmole.
Figure 26:	Bird Images from the Splendor Solis, 1582.
Figure 27:	Engraving from *Musaeum Hermeticum*, Frankfurt, 1625.
Figure 28:	*Rosarium Philosophorum*, from an 18th century English manuscript, copy in the library of John Ferguson, Regius Professor of Chemistry, University of Glasgow.
Figure 29:	Illustrations from the *Atalanta fugiens* series, by the 16th century alchemist Michael Maier.
Figure 30:	*The Saturn key*, woodcut Frankfurt 1737.
Figure 31:	*Philosophia Reformata*, Plate 18, Johann Daniel Mylius (1622).
Figure 32:	*Le Mystere Des Cathedrales*, Fulcanelli, Master Alchemist: Esoteric Interpretation of the Hermetic Symbols of the Great Work (1991), C.W. Daniel.
Figure 33:	*Viatorium spagyricum*, Jamsthaler, (1625) Alchemist in the initial *nigredo* state.
Figure 34:	*Viatorium spagyricum*, Jamsthaler (1625) The Nigredo: the death of the old king, exhaling the spiritus and anima.
Figure 35:	*Philosophia Reformata*, Plate 9: The Putrefactio, Johann Daniel Mylius, (1622).
Figure 36:	*Elementa chemicae*, J.C. Barchusen (1718), in Alexander Roob (2003), *Alchemy & Mysticism*, Taschen.
Figure 37:	The Alchemical Steps from Base Matter to Pure Spirit. The spirit escapes from its worldly confinements and ascends the planetary ladder, coming to rest in eternity.
Figure 38:	*Theatrum Chemicum Britannicum*, Elias Ashmole engraving (1652), London. The toad and the serpent represent the polarity of the volatile fire and fixed earth elements. The flying eagle represents the air aspect of the sublimation.
Figure 39:	*Rosarium Philosophorum*, woodcut 8 (1550). From Alexander Roob's 'Alchemy and Mysticism: *The Hermetic Museum*' (1997) The Self Sacrifice of the Pelican.
Figure 40:	A Scholar in His Study ("Faust"), Rembrandt etching, ca.1652.

Illustrations

by the caduceus, the twinned serpent illustrating both the differentiation and union of opposites. The crowned Mercurius figure, stands above, holding the caduceus and staff, or wand. The six planets surround the font.

Figure 51:   *The Reunion of the Soul and the Body at the resurrection*, William Blake, Theological Scribbles (1808)

Figure 52:   *Rosarium Philosophorum* (1550).

Figure 53:   Rebis from *Theoria Philosophiae Hermeticae* (1617) by Heinrich Nollius.

Front Cover
Sleeping Man from *The Mutus Liber*,or Mute Book, a hermetic philosophical work published in La Rochelle in 1677and one of the major books on alchemy of its time. It has been reprinted numerous times. This illustration is from the 3rd edition, date unknown but probably mid 18th century. www.alchemywebsite. com.

Glossary

albedo

A state of 'whiteness' – one of the colours representing the stages of the alchemical process – black, white, yellow and red. Psychologically *albedo* is analogous to inflation an abstract idealised state, and needs to be transformed by the 'redness', *rubedo* or blood into fully human existence.

alembic

The glass phial or retort within which the alchemical transformations take place. The alembic would be hermetically sealed in order to bring about the death of the *prima materia* through suffocation.

anima mundi

The soul of the world, imprisoned in matter, which the alchemists were attempting to set free.

anthropos

The human manifestation of the philosophers' stone.

aqua permanens

The universal solvent, the liquid form of the philosophers' stone. Also known as the *elixier vitae*, or *aqua vitae*, the divine water of life. Associated with the Moon, as the source of dew – an agent of healing grace.

calcinatio

The fire operation, associated with the transits of Pluto. The intense heating of the material to drive off all volatile constituents. Psychologically, an ordeal or baptism by fire, the stimulation and frustration of desirousness, which demands the endurance of intense affect. A purifying and purging fire which liberates the divine powers from the darkness of matter.

circulatio

Psychologically, the repeated circuit of all aspects of one's being [transits], which gradually generates awareness of a transpersonal centre – the Self – which unites the conflicting factors, and leads to their reconciliation.

coagulatio

The earth operation associated with the transits of Saturn. The material [birth chart] is concretised by the development of the ego. Psychologically, the *coagulatio* corresponds with periods of melancholy, as we realise

Glossary

the weight and limitations of our incarnation, of the
body and flesh.

coniunctio
The greater *coniunctio* is known as the *mysterium
coniunctionis*, the *hieros gamos*, the supreme
accomplishment of the final union of purified opposites,
the marriage of the alchemical king and queen, *sol* and
luna, heaven and earth.

ego
See Self

filius macrocosmi
See *Mercurius*

individuation
The quest for wholeness guided by the human soul.

kairos
The astrologically correct moment when time
intersects with eternity, and the chemical operations
can be successful.

lapis
See philosophers' stone.

massa confusa
See *prima materia*

Mercurius
The autonomous spirit of the archetypal psyche, the
paradoxical manifestation of the transpersonal Self,
which presides over the entire *opus*. The spirit within
matter. Personified as a dragon, serpent or uroboros,
Mercurius divides and unites the opposites and mediates
between the animal, mineral and vegetable realms.

mortificatio
See *nigredo*

mysterium coniunctionis The mystical marriage of opposites. See *coniunctio*

nigredo
A state of 'blackness'. One of the colours representing the
stages of the alchemical process – black, white, yellow
and red. Symbolised by a crow or raven, the *nigredo*
corresponds psychologically to the death of the ego, or
ruling principle of consciousness, and confrontation
with the shadow. *Mortificatio* and *putrefactio* are aspects
of the *nigredo*, felt as deep melancholy, darkness, defeat
and torture. *Putrefactio* is the process of decay, rotting
and decomposition. Psychologically, the corpse, the
old ego identity, has died and must be properly buried.

xiii

opus	The great work, the *magnum opus*, is the central theme of alchemy. The search for the supreme and ultimate value, requiring patience, courage and a religious attitude. Psychologically, the *opus* is analogous to individuation, a process guided by the Self, rather than by the will of the ego.
philosophers' stone	The goal of the *opus* and the final goal of individuation. A miraculous substance, the elixir of life, the universal medicine or panacea. The realisation of the Self, the incarnation of the divine in nature and in mankind. Incorruptible noble matter, the spiritual gold. Once created, the philosophers stone has the power to multiply itself in the alchemical *multiplicatio*. The hidden spiritual power miraculously influences others and generates auspicious reciprocal effects.
prima materia	The first matter, the original fertile chaos, undifferentiated, unconscious potential, without boundaries, limits or forms. The alchemical *opus* begins with the *prima materia* – out of which the ego structure emerges.
psyche	Greek word (*anima* in Latin), meaning soul, spirit, breath, life or animating force. It also means 'butterfly', a creature which goes through a profound metamorphosis. An intermediary and liminal dimension of existence, mediating between the spirit and the body. Using the languages of the imagination, fantasy, myth and metaphor, the *psyche* is a vast memory store which is both personal and collective, known as the soul of the world, the *anima mundi*, more recently as the collective unconscious, and throughout alchemy as *Mercurius*. In the *psyche* we encounter our personal daemons, the carriers of our destiny, which remember the innate image and pattern [birth chart] which determines the course of our lives. See Self.
	In contradistinction to its inclusion in the words psychology, psychotherapy and psychopathology, which generally seek to understand human nature from an objective, empirical, medical and scientific point of view.

Glossary

putrefactio See *nigredo*

quinta essentia The fifth element, quintessence or aether. The universal agent, the combined essence of the three worlds – material, psychic and spiritual. Another word for the philosophers' stone.

sapientia dei Practical wisdom, the feminine face of God, personified as Sophia.

Self The directive centre of the psyche, a central energy field of totality and wholeness which transcends our powers of comprehension. The deity within, the origin of our entire psychic life, felt as a compulsion, our personal daemon. A central guidance system intent on the fulfilment of our predestined wholeness, our given, *a priori*, pattern [the birth chart]. The Self is the unknown and unknowable partner of consciousness, communicating through dreams, myths, symbols and synchronicities.

The Self embraces, includes and sustains the ego. But whereas the ego seeks to preserve the status quo of the personality and its value systems, the Self is often intent on change and re-evaluation, seeming to threaten or challenge the established ego order. The Self urges the ego's transformation.

separatio The separation of a substance [birth chart] into its component parts, by division into two, three and four, as in the tetractys.

solutio The water operation associated with Neptune and its transits. As the material is dissolved, it gives rise to images and dreams of water, floods, tidal waves and swamps. Psychologically, the fixed, static aspects of the personality are returned to their original, undifferentiated state – that is, to the prima materia. A descent into the unconscious, surrender, self dissolution, drowning, blissful regression, ecstacy, fragmentation and dismemberment. An ordeal by water, a return to the womb and the tomb, in preparation for rebirth and baptism in the font of life.

solve et coagula   Dissolve and coagulate, a procedure which is central to alchemy and must be repeated many times, in the *circulatio*, as consciousness and the unconscious instincts confront each other, gradually leading to greater awareness and the capacity to tolerate, and be contained within, the opposites.

soror mystica   The alchemist's female assistant, representing his collaboration with his own feminine side, with his soul.

sublimatio   The air operation associated with the transits of Uranus. The material is volatised and elevated, translated into a higher form by an ascending movement, passing directly into a gaseous state. Images of birds and of flying, fleeing the earth and being transported to heaven. Psychologically, the *sublimatio* process describes the intellect, the ability to reflect, to see things objectively, symbolically. Extreme *sublimatio* symbolises the severing of the mind from the body, a psychological state of dissociation or physical death.

unio mentalis   the first stage of the *coniunctio*, a spiritualising process, the reunion of spirit and soul accompanied by a separation from the body and from nature. The transcendance of earthly life and desires.

Acknowledgements

My interest in the relationship between astrology and alchemy was originally inspired in the late 1980s by a remarkable seminar given by Liz Greene at the Centre for Psychological Astrology, later published in Volume 2 of *Dynamics of the Unconscious* (Red Wheel, Weiser, 1 Nov 1988). This is a subject which has continued to fascinate me for over thirty years, and one which I have kept coming back to.

It was Jung who initially recognised and drew out the links between alchemy and psychology, and three of his collected works are devoted to this subject. His posthumously published *Red Book: Liber Novus* (2009) is itself a powerfully alchemical work. But there is an equally strong synergy between alchemy and astrology and, in my own experience and in my ongoing work with clients, sometimes over several years, I have been fortunate enough to witness the emotional and psychological truths of the alchemical processes. I have no doubt that they lend deeper insight and additional levels of meaning to astrological work and enhance the potential for positive personal growth and healing.

This book also owes a huge debt of gratitude to those brilliant scholars of the soul who have continued to interpret Jung's alchemical work and to make it more accessible.

I have continued to be informed and inspired by Mircea Eliade's seminal work on alchemy: The Forge and the Crucible and, not least, by the writings of Marie-Louise von Franz, James Hillman, Anne Baring, Barbara Somers, Edward Edinger and others, including the large collection of alchemical resources provided by Adam McLean on his website www.alchemywebsite.com. The recent publication of Peter Kingsley's book Catafalque, has completed the circle for me.

I presented a weekend seminar on the subject in 2016, at the Faculty of Astrological Studies' Summer School at Exeter College, Oxford. It was the generous reception of the delegates, their creative engagement with the material and their wonderful contributions which emboldened me to write this book, and I thank them wholeheartedly.

Introduction

The word *alchemy* is commonly used to describe how, when two entities or energies come into contact, both are changed by the encounter, and a new entity, or third force, is created.

The four pillars of western esotericism – alchemy, astrology, hermeticism and the kabbalah – share the common belief that the universe is alive, active and fundamentally inter-actional. In other words, we live in an intelligent, participatory universe which responds to our engagement with it.

> "The planetary deities are spirit beings and inhabitants of the sky. Each spirit seeks its own earthly embodiment – wants to be concretely actualised in the conscious experience of an individual ego."[1]

Astrologers are in constant dialogue with nature, and dialogue is a two-way process of alignment. Astrology unites the eternal and the temporal, invokes the planetary gods and squares the circle. Reading a horoscope is a ritual process of divination in which, if the alchemy is activated, both parties are changed.

In the act of constructing a horoscope the astrologer imposes structure and form onto the cosmic background. The universe is no longer in its natural state, unknown, unseen, unconscious; the natural order of things has been tampered with. The act of creating a personal relationship with the heavenly bodies brings about a change of awareness and sets the scene for the metamorphosis of both the observer and the observed.

Every astrological act of identification, such as the specific position and condition of a planet, its angular relationship to other planets and to the diurnal wheel, extends our understanding of the human psyche, awakens and accelerates the evolution of its expression and contributes to the growth of consciousness. Each insight gained can, and often does, act as a catalyst which continues to reverberate for many years, if not for a lifetime.

> "Each individual is, to a greater or lesser extent, a participant in cosmic creation. Every human experience, to the extent that it is lived in awareness, augments the sum total of consciousness in the

universe. This fact provides the meaning for every experience and gives each individual a role in the on-going world drama of creation."[2]

The birth chart is exactly the same at death as it was at birth and so the important question is what, if anything, has happened? Has the individual's life made an essential difference? If the purpose of human life is the creation of consciousness then, as the alchemists knew, "the sum total of consciousness created by each individual in his lifetime is deposited as a permanent addition in the collective treasury of the archetypal psyche."[3]

The myth of alchemy tells us that consciousness is born out of the experience of opposites, symbolised by spirit and matter, *sol* and *luna*, and personified as the alchemical king and queen. The alchemical *opus* describes how the *prima materia*, or original state of unconscious wholeness, is initially divided, rent asunder, and how, through a series of operations, the opposites are reunited in the *mysterium coniunctionis*, or mystical marriage, in the realisation of conscious wholeness. The product of this union is a mysterious and powerful entity known as the philosophers' stone, in which the experience of the opposites is suffered, not blindly, but in living awareness.

An alchemical approach lends a particular purpose and method to the practice of contemporary psychological astrology. This book explores how astrology might align itself with the long tradition of western mystical alchemy, as a science of the soul, as an initiatory art in which each individual becomes a carrier of consciousness, a vessel for the incarnation of transpersonal meaning.

The alchemists knew that their work on the *prima materia* had a catalytic effect, not just on themselves, but also on their environment. "The implication is that the whole world is in a great process of psychological evolution; it's like a vast alchemical vessel."[4]

Astrology as an alchemical opus

Astrology describes the eternal truths embedded in the cosmos and in our human design. The alchemists believed that the universe was essentially one undivided whole, an *unus mundus*, in which both matter and psyche participate.

Reaching back from the twenty first century into the archaic world of the alchemists takes astrologers into curiously familiar and compelling territory, since the writings and illustrations of the alchemists have a profoundly astrological content. Alchemical works are often contradictory, obscure and difficult to understand, but they appear to describe an imaginative and startlingly visual landscape of the human psyche.

The illustrations found throughout the alchemical texts are powerful, evocative and frequently grotesque and disturbing. But they awaken the imagination, they sink in and we remember them. Alchemical images, like astrological symbols, are open to many different levels of interpretation, but can be understood as originating from the depths of the human psyche, from beyond the personal, from the world of archetypal principles – from the gods. Astrologers can read these images better than most since, again and again, they reflect the structure of the horoscope.

The Rediscovery of Alchemy
Alchemy is just as relevant now as it has always been. Its symbolism, which has evolved over thousands of years, transcends individual experience and cultural norms. Its categories and forms describe the timeless structures which underlie human experience.

Alchemy re-emerged in the twentieth century in a new context, within the soul. Marie Louise von Franz writes that it was Jung "who practically dug alchemy up from the dunghill of the past, for it was a forgotten and despised field of investigation."[5] He discovered, "absolutely empirically", that alchemical themes and images were still very much alive within the human psyche, often emerging spontaneously in the dreams and visions of patients who consciously knew nothing about it.

It was Jung's forty-year labour of love, as he studied the writings of the alchemists through the ages, which provided him with the historical anchor and, most significantly, the language, with which to communicate the discoveries he made about the nature of the human psyche.

Jung's own alchemical journey began in 1913 with his critical descent into the unconscious. He realised that his experiences were the same as the experiences of the alchemists, and the other way around.[6] He recognised that, in their work on the mysterious darkness of the material in their alembics, the alchemists were exploring the images and categories of their own souls. *The Red Book* is a remarkably alchemical work, charting Jung's own inner journey into the realms of the soul and describing his direct encounters with inner figures from myth, the bible and from history, bringing them to life, as the alchemists did, with extraordinary visual images.

Just as the alchemists translated the contents of their souls onto the material in their alembics, so astrologers work with the birth chart, where the material can be seen, reflected upon and interacted with. Alchemical and astrological symbolism, therefore, provides a window into the unconscious, which is profoundly relevant to the work of soul retrieval, psychological growth and healing.

Initiation

Mircea Eliade writes that, without a shadow of doubt, the alchemists' intense participation in the phases of the *opus* was deliberately intended to reflect the ordeals of initiation.

> "The alchemical operations reflect the symbolic processes of dismemberment, death and rebirth which are the fundamental pattern of all initiations and which have to be accomplished over and over again in the tremendous struggle for greater consciousness."[7]

An alchemical approach to astrological work therefore involves deliberately embracing and enduring the various stages of the *opus* as we gradually begin to come home to our deepest selves, to the most fundamental understanding of our own natures, and of the nature of the cosmos, the essence of which is already present within our birth charts. Everything is there right at the beginning; it is just a question of realizing there is nowhere else to go.

Living and working with astrology and with the changing patterns and unfolding cycles of the planets, has a powerful cumulative effect. Gradually, we discover that we have embarked on a personal metamorphosis which brings about a new view of the universe and of the world. Old assumptions and identifications die, and we find ourselves reborn into a profoundly new way of being, now connected with the whole and with life in general, conscious of ourselves as both individual and universal.

Just as the initiatory path is not for everyone, an alchemical approach is not for the faint hearted. It demands conscious endurance and periods of suffering, but it gradually heals the polarised perceptions which have made us strangers from ourselves, from each other and from the world.

Alchemy and astrology retain at their core the knowledge of the age-old wisdom traditions which track the call to adventure. The call is just as potent now as it has always been, but we no longer have the mythic or cultural contexts within which to place it, so it is either ignored completely, pathologised or medicated in cultures which no longer recognise its pressing demands. The journey now has to take place within the individual soul and, as in the case of all initiations, in the belief that the process will be witnessed and guided by unseen forces and influences. Alchemists and astrologers are engaged in transpersonal work, which requires a level of trust that, at the heart of the experience is something which is intelligent, alive and full of energy, participating in the process.

If we have the courage to stay with the process, to keep the alchemical fires burning and enter ever more deeply and imaginatively into its symbolism, the undoubted struggles of the astrological *opus* gradually lead to greater self awareness and, with the acceptance of grace, the development within the individual of increased knowledge, wisdom and compassion which, as the alchemists knew, has a healing effect that spreads throughout the world.

The final stage in all personal initiations is to complete the circle and return to the world, to share with others the insights and gifts received on the journey. In a time which seems to have lost any meaningful myths and severed its connection with the mysteries, the soul of astrology needs to be returned to the world, since it demonstrates that, without doubt, our lives are not, after all, chaotic, meaningless or random.

> "Alchemy is a very simplifying process. A person comes out of it more ordinary, yet where that person goes things are touched and redeemed. He or she can go out into the market-place. They are recognised by their ordinariness, and their joyfulness. Befriending our own divinity we see divinity everywhere."[8]

Astrology, then, is not just an empirical science, charting the measurable relationships between the positions of the planets and physical events on earth. Neither is it just a philosophical construct or intellectual exercise, nor simply a mythic journey of the imagination. It is also a depth psychology of the soul which, to the extent that it is embodied, stimulates real physical and emotional change. The myth of alchemy shows us how.

> "The gods we have lost are descending on us, demanding reconnection. The spirits of alchemy – the symbolic images that have come down to us – are asking for their earthly counterparts – that is, their meaningful realization in modern experience."[9]

Endnotes

1. Edinger, E.F. *Anatomy of the Psyche*, pp.4-5.
2. Edinger, E.F. *The Creation of Consciousness and the Myth of the Anthropos*, p.32.
3. ibid p.57.
4. Edinger, E.F. *The Mysterium Lectures*, p.185.
5. Von Franz, M-L. *Alchemy*, p.14.
6. Kingsley, P. *Catafalque*, p.328.
7. Baring, A. *The Dream of the Cosmos*, p.465.
8. Somers, B. *The Fires of Alchemy*, p.155.
9. *Anatomy of the Psyche*, pp.4-5.

The Alchemical Mountain

Figure 1
The cave of the ancients

This figure illustrates the essential relationship between alchemy and astrology. The alchemist, or blindfolded initiate, is being led into the rabbit hole at the base of the alchemical mountain, to embark on the many stages of the *magnum opus*. The entire process takes place within the zodiac and the four elements, with the seven planets standing on the mountain. Mercury, in the form of *mercurius*, takes pride of place among the seven planets. In the secret chamber the cosmic opposites, the king and queen, are separated and eventually reunited as the alchemical *sol* and *luna*, realised in the triumph of the reborn phoenix.

Chapter 1

Alchemy and Astrology: A Shared Approach

"Truly, without deception, certain and most true. What is below is like that which is above, and what is above is like that which is below, to accomplish the miracles of the one thing."[1]

From the earliest times it was believed that the development of metals within the earth was influenced by the heavens. For alchemists and astrologers, the heavens and the earth belong to the same living soul of creation. Just as the metals upon which alchemists work are the earthly form of the planets, so the planets upon which astrologers work are the heavenly form of the metals.

The ancient correspondences between the planets and the metals are shown in the table below. The Sun and Moon take pride of place, as physical reflections of the sacred metals of gold and silver, the archetypes of spirit and matter. Mercury, or quicksilver, is the physical reflection of mercurius, the archetype of soul. The four elements necessary for life are described by the four cardinal signs of Libra (air), Aries, (fire), Cancer (water) and Capricorn (earth) and, through their rulerships, by the copper of Venus, the iron of Mars, the tin of Jupiter and the lead of Saturn.

Alchemical Planetary Correspondences

Spirit, Soul, Matter

☉	Sun	Gold	[Spirit]	[Sulphur]
☽	Moon	Silver	[Matter]	[Salt]
☿	Mercury	Quicksilver	[Soul]	[Mercurius]

The Four Elements – Cardinal Signs

♀	Venus	Copper	[Libra]	[Air]
♂	Mars	Iron	[Aries]	[Fire]
♃	Jupiter	Tin	[Cancer]	[Water]
♄	Saturn	Lead	[Capricorn]	[Earth]

1

Metals were believed to undergo a natural metamorphosis, developing in the earth over time and becoming more perfect with age. It was the task of the alchemists to assist nature to bring her progeny – be it mineral, vegetable, animal or human – to its supreme ripening.

There is an important idea in alchemy that it is an *opus contra naturam* – a work contrary to nature. In other words, alchemy is a process begun by nature, but which requires the conscious art and effort of a human being to bring to completion. The alchemists believed they were collaborating with the work of nature, assisting her to give birth more rapidly. In their furnaces and retorts, they appropriated fire from the ancient gods of the forge and pursued the promethean vision of speeding up the natural processes.

Figure 2
An alchemist at work in his laboratory

The alchemists were amongst the finest scholars in western European history,[2] many of whom offered up their whole lives to the quest for the philosophers' stone. It is clear that, for the most part, the alchemists were not literally concerned with transforming lead into physical gold, since the phrase 'our gold is not the common gold' is found throughout the alchemical texts. Rather, they were seeking the true, noble or spiritual gold which was the symbol for the realisation of an awakened consciousness of the unity of all creation.

It was the attitude of open curiosity and enquiry which placed the European alchemists, who were mostly educated men and women of the church, within the hermetic tradition of those who sought direct, inner experience rather than adhering exclusively to the dogmas of orthodox Christianity. In that sense, what they were doing was subversive, since they believed that the living spirit, the spiritual gold, was already immanent within all of creation, within every metal, plant, human being and planet. They believed that God was in the process of becoming and needed the assistance of mankind to bring this about. "For the alchemist, man is seen as creative: he redeems nature, masters time, in sum, perfects God's creation."[3] These ideas were religious heresy but are central to the hermetic traditions.

An alchemical approach seeks to release the latent potential which resides within the individual and within the cosmos. There was never any question that the work of the alchemists depended upon a knowledge of the planets and their cycles, since alchemical transformations could only be successful if carried out at the astrologically appropriate times.

The Emerald Tablet

The Egyptians are considered to be the founders of European alchemy, preserving the more ancient knowledge of material properties which was part magic, part religion and part science, but it was the invading Greek, and then the Arabic/Islamic and Jewish cultures that conserved it. Alchemy spread throughout the Islamic world, and in Spain it mixed with other influences, such as kabbalism. From the early 1100s, and throughout the remainder of the 12th century, the corpus of Islamic alchemical works was translated into latin, and alchemy worked its way north into Southern France taking hold throughout Europe by the middle of the 13th century.

In the western tradition, alchemy and astrology took new shape in the writings of the mythical Hermes Mercurius Trismegistus. *The Corpus Hermeticum* is a collection of Greek texts written during the 2nd and 3rd centuries AD, comprising all the texts ascribed to Hermes-Thoth, and believed to be the remnants of a more extensive literature. It was compiled by Italian scholars during the Renaissance, notably Marsilio Ficino, who translated them into latin. Framed as ancient wisdom, these hermetic writings contain the Emerald Tablet,[4] which became

Figure 3
Hermes Trismegistus, mythical author of the *Corpus Hermeticum*

the foundation of western alchemical philosophy and practice for the Arabic, Jewish and Christian alchemists. Treated with great reverence and constantly quoted in alchemical writings, the Emerald Tablet was believed to contain the secret of the *prima materia*, its transmutation and the creation of the philosopher's stone.

The alchemists saw the essence of their art as both analytical and synthetic, involving, on the one hand, prolonged periods of patient discrimination, and on the other hand, synthesis, consolidation and integration. Astrological work follows the same approach. In the act of *separatio*, the many paradoxical and contradictory themes in the horoscope are extracted and assessed separately, revealing a range of inherent conflicts, challenges, gifts and potentials. Each planet has an archetypal core, which must be carefully extracted from the layers of contamination, distortion, ancestral and collective influences which have gathered around it. The various astrological timing techniques gradually bring the inherent themes in the natal chart into clearer focus. In a profoundly alchemical passage, Jung wrote that through the coming into being of the conscious self-reflective mind, mankind has become "indispensable for the completion of creation, a second creator of the world, who alone has given to the world its objective existence – and

4

Figure 4
The planetary trees

without which ... it would have gone on in the profoundest night of non-being down to its unknown end. Human consciousness created objective existence and meaning, and man found his indispensable place in the great process of being."[5]

In Figure 4 the planetary trees have their roots in the earth. As the heavens turn, the planetary spirits are spun into the earth in the form of the seven corresponding metals. It was understood that any alterations to the metals, deliberately brought about by the alchemist in the laboratory, would cause identical changes not only in the planetary spirits but also in the alchemist himself. This is the very core of the alchemical principle.

"That which is true in the *superior* is true in the *inferior*. If alchemy be a great spiritual fact, then it is also a great material fact. If it can take place in the universe, it can take place in man; if it can take place in man, it can take place in the plants and minerals. If one thing in the universe grows, then everything in the universe grows. If one thing can be multiplied, then all things can be multiplied, for the superior agrees with the inferior and the inferior agrees with the superior."[6]

Prima Materia

The theme of alchemy begins with the *prima materia*, or *massa confusa*, the state of original fertile cosmic chaos described in so many creation myths across the world. Often portrayed as a tail-eating dragon, or *uroboros*, the *prima materia* contains all unity and multiplicity in a primal, undifferentiated condition of creation. For Jung, this first substance is the Self, the seat of wholeness which pre-exists the creation of the Ego. The precise character of the *prima materia* defies all definition. The 15th century alchemist Ripley writes that: "Each man possesses it, it is everywhere, in you, in me, in all things, in time and in space. It presents itself in base guise and from it springs our *aqua permanens*."[7]

"In the *prima materia* are images of heaven and earth, summer, autumn, winter and spring, male and female. If thou callest this spiritual, what thou doest is probable; if corporeal, thou sayest the truth; if heavenly thou liest not; If earthly, thou has well spoken."[8]

As the alchemists began their *opus* with the *prima materia*, so astrologers begin their work with the birth chart, a mass of unconscious and undifferentiated material in its natural condition, fundamentally in conflict and capable, therefore, only of collective functioning. In other words, the less we know about ourselves, the more predictable our lives will be.

Figure 5
uroboros

But the birth chart carries the secret of our unique pattern and, as we begin to find ourselves in the crowd, we are no longer driven blindly from without or from within, and gradually become capable of individual functioning. The alchemical opus describes a series of processes designed to gradually transform the original chaos into a conscious living whole.

"Natural man is not a 'self' – he is the mass and a particle in the mass, collective to such a degree that he is not even sure of his own ego. That is why since time immemorial he has needed the transformation mysteries to turn him into something, to rescue him from the animal collective psyche. Life that just happens in and for itself is not real life; it is real only when it is known."[9]

The *prima materia* contains both the poison and the medicine, and it was believed that the more virulent the poison, the more powerful is its potential for healing. In other words, it is the inferior, wounded and unconscious parts of the psyche which contain the mystery and hold the seeds of perfection. They are indispensable for the accomplishment of the *opus*.

The alchemists often wrote that 'to make gold you have to have gold', which implies that the highest value is already immanent, hidden within the *prima materia*, within the birth chart. The birth chart represents both the *prima materia* and the *lapis*, the beginning and the end of the work. It is the conscious differentiation and transformation of the birth chart which constitutes the astrological *magnum opus*.

Alembic

Once the alchemists had collected their *prima materia* it would be transferred into a container, a glass phial known as a retort or an alembic. The alembic must be perfectly round, in imitation of the spherical cosmos, since *the influence of the heavenly bodies is necessary for the work*. The alembic is then *hermetically sealed* in order to bring about the death of the *prima materia* through suffocation.

The birth chart gradually crystallises under the light of our awareness. As we come to understand the particular cosmic patterns we were born with, we are no longer limitless – our existence is given its shape and its boundaries, encompassing all the material of a lifetime.

The birth chart is a mirror in which we can see aspects of ourselves and our lives which would otherwise remain clouded, unknown or entirely projected. The alchemical vessel is a symbol for the deliberate frustration of the drive to project our experiences

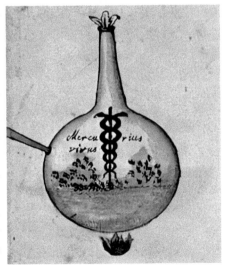

Figure 6
alembic

onto the outside world. Once the alembic has been sealed, we have no option but to stew in our own juice, which can be so painful that we normally try to escape. And yet, it is only through the process of internalisation that we can discover our own souls.

The sealed alembic is analogous to the important task for the astrologer of 'holding the space' – a process well known in psychotherapy – since it is only with the internalisation of the birth chart that real inner changes can start to occur, that the planetary metals within can be purified in the forge until they release the gold within.

Kairos

The concept of *kairos* is central to both alchemy and astrology. Kairos was the ancient Greek god of the fleeting moment, when time intersects with eternity. Kairos is a time in between, the propitious moment for the coming into being of a new state, when something magical can happen. The alchemists knew that chemical processes can only occur at the astrologically right moment.

Astrologers know, for example, that change cannot simply be engineered in the mind. We can decide to change something, but if the *kairos* is not with us, it just won't happen. Change is organic, it has to be experienced emotionally and physically to be real. When the time is right, the inherent nature and specific drive of a particular planet will be intensified by its transits, and then it is possible to actively participate and co-operate with the moment presented. Working in this way, we become co-creators of our lives. We can use the transits of the personal planets to great effect – to seize the day, to push through when Mars, for example, transits our Sun or Ascendant. Or, in the case of the outer planet transits, which may last for up to three years, we can learn to pace ourselves, to enter into their mysterious unfolding and deepen our insights, staying in the kitchen and tending the fire for the duration.

Every time we work to understand how a planet might best function in a particular sign and house, we are adding another atom of consciousness to the way that planet can express itself. Working organically with the kairos, with the transits, gradually deepens our understanding of each planetary archetype, helps us to identify and extract the dross, the ancestral and historical distortions, however obscure, corrupt, suppressed, denied or suffered. Subjecting each planet to the alchemical processes releases the buried planetary archetype to express itself in the most conscious and constructive light, so that it can finally be redeemed and perfected in its expression, both in our own lives and in the celestial vault.

Fire

The alchemists were *masters of fire*, as are many healers, priests, shamans and other specialists in the inner life of the soul. As they applied heat to the base of the sealed alembic, great skill was needed to keep the fire at the right level of intensity. The alchemical operations were difficult and dangerous, with no guarantee of success. Working, as they did, with noxious substances such as mercury and lead, any attempts to force the transformation, driven by greed or ambition, could lead to inflation, madness or death.

The alchemists stressed that the work was to be done gently and patiently, with pure intentions and an attitude of prayer, in service to a source of wisdom greater than their own. They were well aware that, by meddling with the natural order of things, they were intervening in a sacred process, ruled by some higher law. Sensitivity and respect were essential, along with a deep trust in the organic process which is occurring.

Working alchemically, the question is how does the astrologer tend the heat and intensity of each specific transit? Does the fire need to be further kindled or dampened?

Too little heat or intensity means that the process cannot be internalised and the entire meaning of a particular transit will be projected onto outside circumstances or other people. It is only natural to attempt to break the tension by changing external circumstances, such as moving house or changing a job or a relationship, in which case the opportunity for increased self-awareness will be wasted, and the same tensions will re-emerge at another time and in another context.

On the other hand, too much heat and the alembic, or ego container, might break or shatter, causing a breakdown or collapse. The ego must be strong enough – and flexible enough – to contain the process, and we don't know how much pressure the alembic can withstand. "The unconscious can be integrated only if the ego holds its ground."[10]

Figure 7
Alchemist tending the fire

Figure 7 shows the primitive instincts on fire, in the form of a dragon, contained in a cave beneath the earth. Mars, with his bow and arrow indicates the painful condition of this state, but the alchemist, in the guise of Jupiter, holds out his right hand, guiding and overseeing the process. Above the cave is the golden lion, symbolising the spiritual gold which will eventually emerge from this ordeal by fire.

Circulatio

The *opus* was often referred to as *circulare* (circular) or *rota* (wheel), to describe its progress backwards and forwards, separating and connecting, dividing and merging, one after the other, again and again, around and around, reflecting the circular movement of the Sun and the planets through the signs and houses of the zodiac. At any one time there are likely to be separating and unifying processes occurring simultaneously in different, or even in the same, areas of our lives. There is no standard or sequential order in which the alchemical processes occur – it all depends on the birth chart and its unique development, reflected in transits and progressions.

As the planets revolve around the earth, around the birth chart, their circular and spiral movements bring burnings and cleansings, expansions and contractions, progressions and regressions, gradually spinning the web of our lives. The *circulatio* describes our ever deepening discovery of what has been there from the beginning, in the *prima materia*, but unknown.

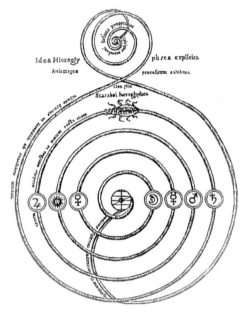

Figure 8
The *circulatio*

"This goes on constantly with psychological understanding; there are many layers and something can always be understood on a new and deeper level. You understand it with a part of yourself and then the penny drops deeper, as it were, and you realize the same thing but in a more living and rich way than before. That is what I find so beautiful about this work – it is an adventure which never comes to an end, for each time you turn a corner a completely new vista of life opens; you never know and have it all settled."[11]

Endnotes
1. *The Emerald Tablet*, see Appendix I.
2. It is worth including the names of just some of these scholars. Albertus Magnus (1193-1280), [Thomas Aquinas (1225-1274)], Roger Bacon (1214-1294), Ramond Lull (1235-1315), Pope John XXII (1249-1334), Arnold of

Villanova (1245-1311), Nicolas Flamel (1330-1418), George Ripley (15th Century), Johann Faust (c.1480-c.1541), Cornelius Agrippa (1486-1535), Paracelsus (1493-1541), John Dee (1527-1609), Gerhard Dorn (c.1530-1584), Tycho Brahe (1546-1601), Edward Kelley (1555-1597), Michael Maier (1568-1622), Jacob Boehme (1575-1624), Elias Ashmole (1617-1692), Robert Boyle (1627-1691), Isaac Newton (1642-1727), Johann Wolfgang Goethe (1749-1832), Rudolf Steiner (1861-1925), Carl Gustav Jung (1875-1961).

3. *Parabola, Inner Alchemy*, Volume III, Number 3, p.20.
4 *The Emerald Tablet*, see Appendix I.
5. Jung, C.G. *Memories, Dreams, Reflections*, pp.240-1.
6. Hall, Manly P. *The Secret Teachings of all Ages: The Theory and Practice of Alchemy*.
7. Quoted by Jung, *Psychology and Alchemy*, p.442.
8. Quoted by Jung, *Mysterium Coniunctionis Tractatus Micreris*, Theatr. Chem., V, p.111, para.7.
9. Jung, C.G. (CW12) *Psychology and Alchemy*, p.81.
10. Jung, C.G. *The Psychology of the Transference*, p.132.
11. Von Franz, M-L. *Alchemy*, p.257.

Chapter 2

Number Symbolism in Alchemy and Astrology

"And as all things proceeded from one, through mediation of the one, so all things come from this one thing through adaptation."[1]

Number symbolism is fundamental to both alchemy and astrology. In his work with patients, Jung discovered that images produced by the unconscious have a mathematical structure, revealing something about the way our minds are constructed, about the way we interpret the world. As an archetype of cosmic order, number symbolism provides a common language with which to explore alchemy, astrology, the kabbalah and, of course, the structure of the human psyche.

Pythagoras and his followers believed that the nature of all things could be understood according to the powers of the one, the two, the three and the four as an unfolding sequence of creation. The mathematical model they devised is known as the tetractys, one of the most deceptively simple and yet profound models that exists in the western tradition. The Pythagoreans believed that the tetractys described the nature and structure of the universe and of every system within it, including the human being.

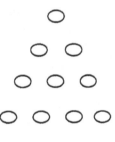

Figure 9
The *tetractys*

The tetractys not only describes the various stages of the alchemical opus, but also the identical processes in the development of consciousness within the individual and within the collective.

"Man, by comprising a world-order in miniature, contains all of those principles constituting the greater cosmos, of which he is a reflection, including the powers of divinity. Man realises the divine by knowing the universal principles which constitute the cosmos - i.e. for the Pythagoreans, Number. To know the cosmos is to seek and know the divine within, since only like can know like."[2]

Astrologers are already familiar with the symbolism of the tetractys, since it exactly reflects the structure of the horoscope. The circle is a

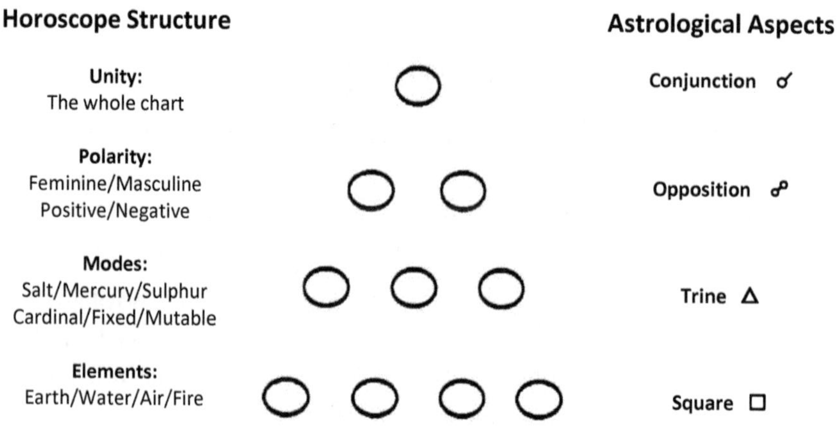

Horoscope Structure   **Astrological Aspects**

Unity:
The whole chart   O   Conjunction ☌

Polarity:
Feminine/Masculine   O   O   Opposition ☍
Positive/Negative

Modes:
Salt/Mercury/Sulphur   O   O   O   Trine △
Cardinal/Fixed/Mutable

Elements:
Earth/Water/Air/Fire   O   O   O   O   Square ◻

Figure 10
The structure of the horoscope

symbol of wholeness, of the eternal spirit, which contains all of creation. The point in the centre of the birth chart represents the potential for the consciousness of wholeness. Each sign of the zodiac is simultaneously polar (active or passive), modal (cardinal, fixed or mutable) and elemental (fire, earth, air, water). The astrological interpretations of the conjunction, opposition, trine and square derive from this same model.

The Axiom of Maria Prophetessa

One of the most famous alchemists was Mary the Jewess, also known as Maria Prophetessa. Although none of her writings have survived, quotations credited to her are found in numerous hermetic and alchemical texts. She is said to have invented several kinds of chemical apparatus (such as the bain-marie) and to have spoken of the union of opposites: 'Join the male and the female, and you will find what is sought'. She is also known for her famous 'axiom of Maria', of which there are several versions:

"One becomes two, two becomes three, and out of the third comes the One as the fourth."[3]

"One and it is two; two and it is three; three and it is four; four and it is three; three and it is two; two and it is one."[4]

14

Figure 11
Maria Prophetessa

The axiom of Maria is constantly referred to in alchemical works, "running like a *leitmotiv* throughout almost the whole of the lifetime of alchemy, extending over more than seventeen centuries".[5] For Jung, it was a summary of the individuation process.

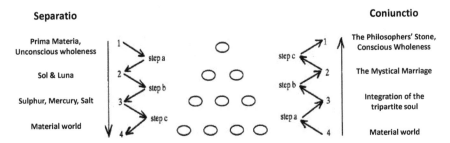

Figure 12
The stages of the *magnum opus*

So the sequence goes: one, two, three, four; four, three, two, one. Working down the tetractys, the initial task is the *separatio*, the extraction and differentiation of each level of creation – spirit, soul and body – since, as the alchemists repeatedly stated, *only separated things can unite*.

Throughout the alchemical illustrations, spirit, soul and body are graphically represented by the circle, the triangle and the square. This engraving, from Michael Maier's *Atalanta Fugiens* (1618), shows the alchemist at work, and is accompanied by the following text:

15

Figure 13
Alchemist at work

"Here follows the Figure conteyning all the secrets of the Treatise, both great and small. Make a circle out of a man and woman, derive from it a square, and from the square a triangle: make a circle and you will have the philosopher's stone."

The Four Elements

"Its father is the sun; its mother the moon; the wind has carried it in its belly; its nurse is the earth. This is the father of all, the completion of the whole world. Its strength is complete if it be turned into earth."[6]

Figure 14

Earth   Water   Air   Fire

The number four symbolises manifestation, matter and substance. The birth chart is identical to the symbol for the Earth, the cross within the circle, or the spirit made manifest, and describes the specific nature and circumstances of the material world into which each of us is born, since the word *nature* means 'that which is born'.

The Greeks considered that every living thing was made up of some combination of earth, water, air and fire; cold, wet, dry and hot; substance, moisture, respiration and light, or, in modern terminology, solid, liquid, gas and plasma. The four elements combined in various proportions to create life itself, an idea which became a cornerstone of philosophy, science and medicine for two thousand years. During life, the four elements are held together by the *quinta essentia*, the spirit, or life force itself, which permeates all of nature.

Figure 15
mandala

At death, the soul is released from the body and the four elements return to their origins. These ideas belong to the Hermetic and neo-Platonic schools of thought and have been carried down through the ages by the wisdom traditions.

A balance of the elements within the individual was considered necessary for physical and psychological health, and a marked imbalance the cause of distress and disease. These concepts gave rise to the development of the four humours, or temperaments, in Greek medicine, a system of classification which was used throughout medieval and renaissance Europe.

Drawing on the ancient tradition of the fourfold nature of matter, Jung believed that the number four, or the quaternity, provides a description of the way the conscious mind takes its bearings. A real adaptation to the world requires the differentiation of the psychological functions of intuition, sensation, thinking and feeling.

"This task entails the most painstaking self-examination and self-education. The process of psychological differentiation is no light work; it needs the tenacity and patience of the alchemist who must purify the body from all superfluities in the fiercest heat of the furnace."[7]

Coniunctio

The return journey is described in the three stages of the *coniunctio*, leading to the completion of the *opus*, the realisation of the *lapis*, or *philosophers' stone*, the primordial oneness which lies beneath or beyond our human experiences of conflict and fragmentation. All levels of existence are equally honoured, valued and included without sacrificing their distinctiveness, and the reconciled spirit/soul/body is united with the world in conscious wholeness.

> "Thus has the world been created. From here will come the marvellous adaptations, whose manner this is."[8]

Endnotes

1. *The Emerald Tablet*, see Appendix I: para.3.
2. K.S. Guthrie (1987), *Pythagorean Source Book and Library*, p.32.
3. Jung, C.G., CW12 *Psychology and Alchemy*, par.209.
4. ibid, par.210, footnote 86.
5. ibid, par.26.
6. *The Emerald Tablet*, see Appendix 1: paras.4-6.
7. Jung, C.G., CW12 *Psychology and Alchemy*, p.132.
8. *The Emerald Tablet*, see Appendix I: paras.10 & 11.

Chapter 3
The Stages of the Magnum Opus

"And as all things proceeded from one, though mediation of the one,
so all things come from this one thing through adaptation."[1]

Polarity and Projection

Duality emerges out of the original unity in what is known as the 'primal
schism', or the 'separation of the world parents'. The creation myths
of almost every culture describe the first division out of the primordial
ocean, or chaos, which creates by dividing itself, in the same way that a
living cell divides and becomes two.

Astrologically, the symbolic separation of the world parents occurs
at the moment of birth: the ASC/DES axis separates the heavens and
the earth, day and night, or Ouranos and Gaia, the original parents of
Greek myth symbolised by Uranus (clarity and detachment) and Pluto
(the chthonic, organic life force). Simultaneously we are quartered and
made mortal by the MC/IC axis which separates east from west, the
daily rising and setting of the sun and, by analogy, birth from death.
Being simultaneously divided and quartered by the angles, we become
oriented in time and space by the co-ordinates in our birth charts.

Each astrological sign is either positive or negative, active or passive,
masculine or feminine, and each planet (with the exception of the
Sun and Moon) has rulership over both a positive and negative sign.
Oppositions are aspects of maximum instability, and the four angles and
six sign axes describe the tension of the inherent duality which defines
our experience of ourselves and of the world. Polarities both repel and
attract each other, and it is out of this tension that awareness is born.

"The phenomenon of opposites constitutes the most basic anatomy
of the collective psyche. The flow of libido, or psychic energy,
is generated by the polarization of opposites in the same way as
electricity flows between the positive and negative poles of an
electrical circuit. The opposites are truly the dynamo of the psyche.
They are the motor, they are what keeps the psyche alive."[2]

19

Dane Rudhyar wrote that: "it simply does not make any sense to try and define the meaning of one end of an axis without including in the definition the meaning of the other end."[3] Thus, the meaning of the sign Aquarius includes Leo, Aries includes Libra, that of Taurus includes Scorpio, and so on, just as the roles we play in life demand their opposites; every child needs a parent, every student needs a teacher and every rescuer needs an invalid, and vice versa. Whenever we are consciously polarised at one end of an axis, we force 'the other' to live out the opposite, unconscious, pole for us.

The Astrology of Relationships

The natal chart describes with great accuracy the nature of our relationships to ourselves, other people and with the world. We instinctively gravitate towards situations and other people who will carry and reflect back to us the unconscious contents of our own souls. This is why relationships cannot be looked at 'objectively', since, generally speaking, they are founded on projection and we are not capable of relating to other people as they actually are. But this also explains why relationships are essential in our journey towards increased self-knowledge and personal integration, since we cannot do that alone, in a vacuum.

Once a relationship is constellated and the relationship alembic is sealed, our internal conflicts begin to emerge. Dane Rudhyar writes that human experience is forever the outcome of the interplay of consciousness and unconsciousness, of individual and collective. "Wherever the pulse of life is felt, there must be disequilibrium, conflict, strain and the experience of suffering."[4]

Astrologers are in the unique position of being able to identify from the birth chart where the tensions of opposing forces and values reside. They cannot be reconciled until they are made conscious. This is very simple astrology, but extremely useful and practical.

Just as the alchemists would contain the struggle within the pressure of the sealed alembic, so the astrologer's task is to hold the tension of the opposites in the birth chart. This is an uncomfortable and difficult thing to do, and yet a conscious fusion of opposites creates a new psychological reality which is more than the sum of its parts. To the extent that we become conscious of our inner opposites, we no longer have to try and cut off parts of ourselves. This leads to greater self-acceptance, humility, humour, and a reconnection to the paradoxical mysteries of life.

It is only when the opposites can reconnect with their source that they can be mediated and reconciled. This describes the central role of the alchemical *mercurius*.

The Alchemy of Relationships

The alchemical opus begins with the separation of the world parents. Psychologically, this refers to the development of self-awareness, including consciousness of the opposites, out of the previously undifferentiated *prima materia*.

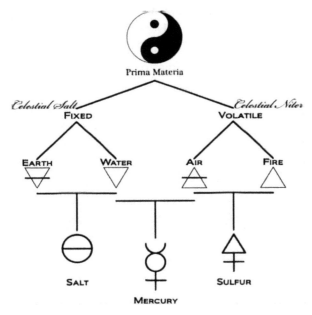

Figure 16
The division of the *prima materia*

In the first stage of the *separatio*, the *prima materia* is divided into the active principle, represented in alchemical images by the Sun, the king, the father, and the passive principle, represented by the Moon, the queen, the mother. Just as the father represents collective consciousness, the traditional spirit, so the mother stands for the collective unconscious, the source of the waters of life.

This is a symbolic description of the fact that all our experiences come through this primal division, through the separation of what the alchemists called the celestial salt and the celestial spirit, or sulphur. As the diagram shows, it is out of this primal separation that the further division into the four elements emerges, the upward pointing triangles of air and fire being expressions of the volatile, or active masculine principle and the downward pointing triangles of earth and water being expressions of the fixed, or passive feminine principle.

Spirit and matter are represented by the opposing alchemical principles of sulphur and salt, and by the astrological principles of Uranus and Pluto. From an archetypal perspective, Uranus is entirely non-biological and Pluto is entirely non-intellectual. As with all opposites, the alchemists understood that each sought the death of the other.

Eventually, once the masculine and feminine principles have been made conscious and separately transformed, the alchemical goal is to reunite them in the *coniunctio*, the ritual union of *sol* and *luna*, king and queen, sulphur and salt, a process mediated by the soul, the alchemical *mercurius*. The ultimate fruit of this union is the birth of the magical child, the *filius philosophorum*, as a symbol of awakened consciousness.

The Marriage of Opposites

The separation, transformation and reunion of the opposites at a new level is a central theme in alchemy, and illustrations of the mystical marriage between the alchemical king and queen are found throughout the alchemical texts.

These remarkable images from the *Rosarium Philosophorum* show the alchemical Sun and Moon, the king and queen, entering into a formal relationship; their encounter is restrained and distant. In the first image, they are crowned and fully dressed. He is standing on the Sun and she on the Moon. With their right hands, representing consciousness, they proffer two-blossomed flowers to each other. But their handshake is left handed, sinister, or dark, signifying that an unconscious reciprocal contract is being formed in the depths of their souls, and indicating that something profound is going to occur. From the spiritual realm above, indicated by the star, the bird of the soul descends, also bearing a two-blossomed flower.

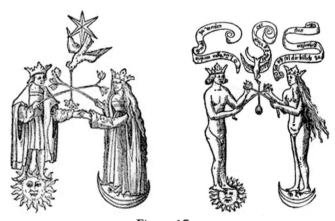

Figure 17
The marriage of the alchemical king and queen

The presence of spirit and soul throughout the alchemical operations demonstrates the theurgical nature of alchemy. Alchemists (and astrologers) who tentatively begin the task of working with the inner opposites, find that they are supported and assisted in their work by the soul and by the gift of spiritual grace.

In the next image, the process has moved one stage further. The court clothes of the king and queen, the 'veils of consciousness', have been removed and the figures are now naked and vulnerable. They have started to see each other more clearly, and their handshake now involves all four hands. The branch held out by the king in his right hand is grasped by the right hand of the queen, while the branch held out by the queen in her left hand is received by the left hand of the king. The branches are now single-blossomed, and from above the dove still bears its unifying branch. The scroll above the king states, "O *luna*, let me be thy husband", while the queen says "O *sol*, I must submit to thee". The dove bears the inscription, "It is the spirit which vivifies".

A similar illustration from the *Anatomia Aurea* shows the formal engagement of the king and queen, *sol* and *luna*, standing on the earth. Mercury on both sides of the alembic represents the union of opposites, and the figure in the alembic symbolises the new life which will result from this union.

Simultaneously, the hidden, instinctual and unconscious nature of this engagement is illustrated by the bird feet beneath the two figures and

Figure 18
The marriage of the alchemical
king and queen

under the earth. For Jung, the most powerful factor in relationships is the attraction via the unconscious. He coined the terms *anima* and *animus* to describe the invisible partners, the unconscious inner opposites which complete the marriage quaternity.

The *anima* and *animus* are numinous archetypes, charged with psychic energy, which tend to grip us emotionally. In every real encounter they are awakened and start to engage. They have a magnetic effect on us, and the person who carries such a projection will tend to greatly attract or repel us. There is nothing individual about such encounters; they are driven by lust and by the will to power, by the desire to incorporate the other, body and soul, or to devour and destroy them. Being unconscious, they are highly destructive to personal relationships. Whenever we fall into an identification with one of a pair of warring opposites, we lose the possibility, for the time being anyway, of being a carrier of the opposites, "and instead we become one of God's millstones that grinds out fate".[5]

> "Consciousness requires a simultaneous experience of opposites and the acceptance of that experience. And the greater the degree of this acceptance, the greater the consciousness."[6]

It is clear from many alchemical illustrations that the alchemists worked alongside female figures, known as their *soror mystica*, or mystical sister, reflecting in the laboratory what was taking place in the flask. Partners in the alchemical work are usually described as brother and sister, mother and son or father and daughter. The incestuous nature of such relationships points to the fact that, in the end, it is a question of achieving an un-projected inner experience of unity and wholeness.

Eventually, if the alchemical work is to proceed, the 'other', who is

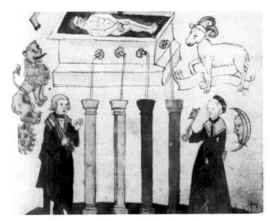

Figure 19
The alchemist with his *soror mystica*, both holding the keys to the work

carrying the burden of all our unconscious expectations, starts to let us down. The person upon whom we have projected the image of ourselves refuses to play the role any more. It is at this point, when relationships become uncomfortable, difficult or threatening, that clients may well consult an astrologer. Their partner may have betrayed them, or become restrictive, demanding, controlling, absent, neglectful, boring, abusive or needy. The fantasy has been pierced, and then the battle begins. But "Consciousness is achieved only through the loss of the Other, and the perception that the Other is truly Other."[7]

In Figure 20, the Sun king is clothed and the Moon queen is naked, signifying the encounter between masculine consciousness and the

Figure 20
The battle between the alchemical king and queen

25

feminine realms of the unconscious. The male is astride a lion, his head is the Sun but there are three moons on his shield. The female sits sideways on the griffin, her head is the Moon but there is an image of the Sun on her shield. The lion and the griffin are opposed, engaging in the battle of the opposites, and they will tear each other to pieces if they can get to each other.

The Death of the Alchemical King and queen

At some point, in any serious and transformational encounter, both parties have to die to their separateness, and they must die again and again in the *circulatio*.

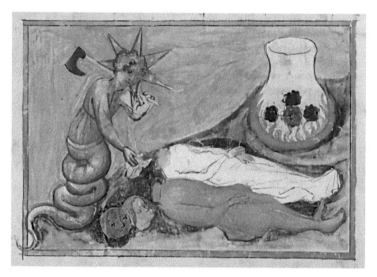

Figure 21
The death of the alchemical king and queen

In Figure 21 *mercurius*, in the form of a serpent, has decapitated the red king and the white queen, the Sun and the Moon, with his axe. As they lie dead in front of him, gold and silver flowers are submitted to alchemical transformation in the vessel on the fire.

Avicenna wrote: "Purify husband and wife separately, in order that they may unite more intimately; for if you do not purify them, they cannot love each other.[8]

In Figure 22 the king and queen lie as if dead in a sepulchre or coffin. A skeleton with a scythe stands by. On the left, the figure of Saturn

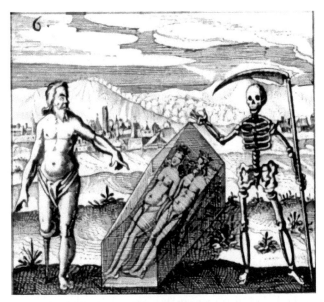

Figure 22
The death of the alchemical king and queen

points to the coffin, indicating that time and patience are needed during this stage.

The king and queen have died to their separateness, and will be separately transformed in the alchemical processes, in preparation for their conscious reconciliation in love, in the greater *solutio*.

In our culture, the spiritual and physical worlds have become different in kind. Mind has been separated from matter, thinking from feeling, intellect from intuition and reason from instinct. The split between creative spirit and chaotic nature, between light and dark, increasingly associated with good and evil, has led to the devaluation of the body and the marginalisation of the feminine. With the focus on the intellect, the goddess has become associated with nature as a chaotic force to be mastered, and the god has taken the role of conquering or ordering nature from his counter-pole of spirit, a development charted in the great creation myths of the western world.

There are, and have always been, aspects of the feminine which are so frightening and uncontrollable that they have been demonised, repressed and consigned to the collective unconscious. The powerlessness of humanity in the face of nature's destructive power is deeply imprinted on the memory of our species, and the devouring aspect of the *great mother* is documented in almost every early mythology.

Jung recognised that the fundamental idea of alchemy points back to the primordial matriarchal world which was overthrown by the masculine world of the father.[9] What has been consciously suppressed does not disappear, and the grotesque and sinister side of the unconscious has remained in its original savage stage for the reason that it has never been integrated. Consigned to the unconscious, "the dark forces of the world, the invisible, all pervading effluences of the spirits of the dead, demons and gods, witches and magicians, show themselves in murderous impulses, emotional outbursts, orgiastic frenzies and psychic epidemics."[10]

Throughout the alchemical writings and illustrations, it is clear that the Sun and Moon, spirit and nature, the masculine and feminine archetypes, have equal value, and they are always given equal weight and significance, as balancing principles. The alchemists understood that their initial polarization was a necessary part of the process of *separatio*, and one which could eventually lead to their conscious reunion, as equals. In this respect alone, the alchemical tradition is of immense importance in our times.

> "Consciousness is an enduring psychic substance which is produced by the experience of opposites suffered, not blindly, but in living awareness."[11]

Alchemy and astrology have been ceaselessly engaged in preserving the bridge to nature. In their attempts to reconnect with the eternal cycles of birth, growth, destruction, decay and new formation, the alchemists, like Faust, descended into the dark and mysterious realm of the Mothers, to the formless primary matter from which all things are born, and, by uniting with nature they sought to consummate the mystical marriage and accomplish their life's work.

Endnotes
1. *The Emerald Tablet*, see Appendix I.
2. Edinger, E.F. *The Mystery of the Coniunctio*, p.11.
3. Rudhyar, D. *The Astrological Houses*, p.154.
4. Rudhyar, D. *The Pulse of Life*, p.144.
5. Jung, C.G. (CW8) *The Structure and Dynamics of the Psyche*, par. 425.

6. Edinger, E.F. *The Mystery of the Coniunctio*, p.12.
7. Hollis, J. *The Eden Project: In Search of the Magical Other*, p.17.
8. Raf, Jeffrey (2003) *The Wedding of Sophia*, quote by Avicenna cited by Edward Kelly.
9. Jung, C.G. (CW12) *Psychology and Alchemy*, par. 26.
10. Neumann, E. *The Origins and History of Consciousness*, p.40.
11. Edinger, E.F. *The Creation of Consciousness and the myth of the Anthropos*, p.32.

Figure 23
The mercurial fountain

This image from the *Rosarium Philosophorum* can be read as a schematic representation of the tetractys and of the birth chart. It shows the mercurial fountain, with three streams flowing from the fountain head, to represent the tripartite soul. In the circular basin with three legs the differentiated soul forces are merged together and the three become one.

The six planets appear on the basin, with Mercury as the seventh, represented both by the star above the fountain and by the double headed serpent or dragon at the top. Mercurius divides and unites the opposites and presides over the animal, mineral and vegetable realms.

The Sun and Moon straddle the mercurial star, as parents of the mystical transformation. The four stars in the corners represent the four elements.

Chapter 4
Alchemy, Astrology and the Soul

The alchemical texts and images reveal that, from the earliest times[1], the alchemists understood that the soul is the vessel in which the mysterious transformations take place. They believed that the fate of the world depended on the individual's capacity to create a loving relationship with his or her soul.

James Hillman spent much of his life calling for a return of the soul to a central place in psychology. He believed that the real tragedy of our modern condition is the increasing focus on the individual and our isolation from the world around us, that: "*The* modern suffering is being only an individual."[2] An individualistic approach cuts us off from the roots of our being, from the 'spirit of the depths' which sustains and supports us. Anxious, restless and alienated, we live on the surface in a world where only the tangible and material is real.

Dane Rudhyar was another visionary who recognised that the development of individualism and ego ambitions was responsible for our increasing alienation from nature and from ourselves. "A new set of problems develops, and today it is the solution of these new problems that is the main task for astrology."[3]

Jung introduced the term *collective unconscious* to describe the vast memory field which embraces the total species and planetary memory. Specific aspects of this vast field are given shape when we are born. They are part of our psychic DNA.

Both Freud and Jung demonstrated that the unconscious has an awareness of its own which is not only different from, but, in certain respects, superior to ego consciousness. Jung believed that the collective unconscious, which he later named the *objective* or non-personal psyche, appears to have an intention for us, making itself known through dreams and intuitions which contain way more than our conscious minds know.

For the Greeks, it was the daemons whose irrational, obsessive impulses arise against our will and take possession of us. We are just as susceptible to daemonic activity as we have always been but, in cultures which do not recognise the reality or truth of the soul, the daemons of old

31

are now treated purely physiologically, as symptoms. Communications from the soul, images, visions and dreams are diagnosed, pathologized or explained away. They have not been demonised so much as medicalised, an observation which caused Jung to comment that "the gods have become diseases."[4]

Alchemy and the Threefold Nature of the Soul

The alchemists were, of course, working with the seven visible planets, bounded by Saturn. And yet it is clear that they were intuitively aware of the principles we now associate with the three outer planets, Uranus, Neptune and Pluto. The outer planets appear to find their place in the alchemical scheme as aspects of the soul.

There is a long tradition of the threefold nature of the soul.[5] One part was believed to be 'spirited', another 'reasoning' and the third desiring the 'pleasures of nutrition and generation'.

The first part is active or positive; the second neutralising, and the third passive or negative. These three forces are recognised throughout the wisdom traditions, as, for example in the three pillars of the kabbalistic tree of life. There is also a striking analogy between the three parts of the soul and the cardinal, mutable and fixed modes in astrology. Seen in this light, the threefold soul-substance is comprised of the masculine, active solar forces [Uranus], the feminine, receptive lunar forces [Pluto], and the water of life, the aqua vitae, or inner source of the mediating soul energies [Neptune].

Known in alchemy as the three philosophical elements, sulphur, mercury and salt were clearly described as principles rather than substances, and "not to be confounded in any way with the crude mercury, sulphur and salt taken from the earth or secured from the apothecary".[6] According to Waite, these three principles exist in all things; without them nature is powerless and nothing can exist or be done. "If, after purging them well, you join them together, they must by a natural process, result in a most pure substance."[7]

Paracelsus' theory, which became known as the *tria prima*, directly equated these three principles with spirit (sulphur), soul (mercury) and body (salt).

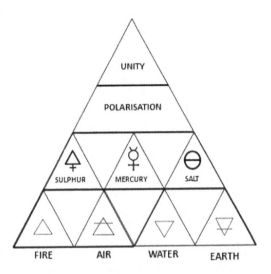

Figure 24
The threefold nature of the soul

"Nature, whose power is in her obedience to the Will of God, ordained from the very beginning that the four elements should incessantly act on one another, so, in obedience to her behest, fire began to act on air, and produced Sulphur; air acted on water and produced Mercury; water, by its action on earth, produced Salt. Earth, alone, having nothing to act upon, did not produce anything, but became the nurse, or womb, of these three Principles."[8]

Paracelsus believed that disease was caused by an imbalance in the body of sulphur, mercury and salt, and that physical and psychic health results when the three parts of the soul are brought into a state of harmony, where each part receives what it is due.

Mercurius

The soul's realm is an invisible and intermediary dimension of existence known traditionally as the *anima mundi*, more recently as the *collective unconscious*, and throughout alchemy as *mercurius*, normally personified in the form of a dragon, serpent or uroboros.

Mercurius presides over the entire opus. Mediating between the spirit and the body, the task of the bipolar mercurial principle of the soul is to separate and reunite the cosmic opposites. He is the beginning, middle

Figure 25
Sun and Moon dragons

and end of the work, the circumference and the centre of the circle, the
prima materia and the *ultima materia*, the goal of his own transformation.

The alchemy scholar Adam McClean[9] suggests that, in our present
state of evolution, there is a vast gulf between the spiritual and physical
realms; they are at war with each other. It is only in the soul that these
primal polarities can be integrated.

In Figure 26, the three aspects of the soul are illustrated in the form
of three birds in the alembic, often coloured black, white and red, which
are initially in a state of turmoil. It was the task of the alchemists to bring
these principles into harmony, the crowned three headed bird symbolising the achievement of a healthy, contented and integrated soul.

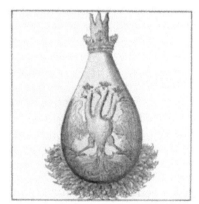

Figure 26
Bird images of the three parts of the soul

34

One of the main tasks of alchemy is to keep soul in the middle, not allowing it to disappear either in the ethereal heights of spirit or in the dense materialism and overwhelming attractions of the body and its world.

The active or cardinal part of the soul is governed by spiritual ideals and motivations. Ideas and concepts can remain abstract, theoretical, ungrounded, detached or dissociated. If they are to become practically or functionally real, they need to be mediated by the soul.

On the other hand, the passive, fixed part of the soul can become lost in the realm of the senses, in which case physical survival becomes the whole point. Many myths describing the incarnation of the soul explain how, at birth, the soul is swallowed by matter, forgets its origins, and comes to believe that the body and the material world are the only reality. "Without soulful fantasy all is profane and secular, a world reduced to serve as fodder for our pragmatic intentions."[10]

One of the most important alchemical tasks was to rescue the soul from its flight into spirit, and to extract soul from its immersion in matter, from the confines of materialism, since it is not *of* matter, but acts upon it.

Once this has been achieved, the task of the alchemist is to bring the three parts of the soul into a new synthesis. An alchemical consciousness speaks to both affections of the soul, spiritualizing what is otherwise dense and literal, and concretizing that which is excessively intellectual or spiritual. The integrated soul is aligned to both masculine spirit and feminine matter, but is lost in neither.

In Figure 27 the seven planetary metals are under the earth, corresponding to the seven planets, shown both above the earth, in the day, and below the earth, at night. In both cases the Sun and Moon straddle the five other planets. The three aspects of soul are represented by the female figures seated on the surface of the earth, beneath trees which symbolise their connection with the above and the below.

The spiritual aspect of the soul is represented by the figure on the left, holding the upward pointing triangle, symbolising the masculine principle, "the dynamism of upward striving, towards the heavens, towards light, air, spirit, abstraction, expansion and rationality."[11] The earthy, material aspect of the soul is represented by the figure on the right, holding the downward pointing triangle, symbolising the feminine

Figure 27
Spirit, soul and matter in harmony

principle, "towards inwardness and incarnation, organic experiencing rather than rational explanation".[12] The central figure holds the masculine and feminine principles combined in the form of a six pointed star, a symbol of perfect harmony, indicating that when these archetypal forces are in balance, everything in the world likewise achieves balance. In the corners of the engraving the elements are represented as the salamander (fire), the cherubim (air), the fish and ship (water) and the landscape (earth).

In Figure 28, the soul is represented by three streams flowing from the mouths of three cherub heads, identified as Spiritus, Anima and Corpus, and labelled with the chemical symbols for mercury, sulphur and salt. They pour into the world, represented by the square container, and their united essence is collected in the alchemical vessel.

Spiritus Anima
vnd Corpus

Figure 28
The three aspects of the soul united

The nodal axis
The nodal axis represents the symbolic meeting place of spirit, soul and matter, since it is here that the Sun, Moon and Earth are in alignment. As such, the nodal axis describes the cosmic struggle of the opposites, the tension of our dual nature, as both spiritual and physical beings. Alchemy teaches us that the polarisation can only be healed in the soul, the mediating principle between opposites.

From an alchemical perspective, the nodal axis represents the potential for the sacred marriage of the masculine and feminine principles, the *mysterium coniunctionis*.

As a spacial axis, the nodes can be understood as the mysterious threshold between this and other worlds or dimensions where, at certain times in our lives, we become aware of meaningful coincidences between inner and outer events, and can sometimes glimpse or sense our soul's purpose and pattern, our *entelechy*, the deeper purpose and function of our existence.[13] In this liminal space, we have access to the vast memory store which is both personal, ancestral and collective, known to the Greeks as the soul of the world, the *anima mundi*. The *anima mundi* is not only 'full of gods', as Proclus[14] wrote, but, astonishingly, it also appears to be interested in us. So we may not be as alone as we think.

It is on this axis that we encounter our daemons, often in the form of other people, animals or mythic beings, who remember our image and our pattern and are therefore the carriers of our destiny. Acting as messengers, guides or mentors, they may inspire, challenge or appear to thwart us, and it is only later that we recognise their role in helping us remember and fulfil our soul's purpose.

Astrology, the Soul and the Outer Planets
The rescue of the individual soul from the weight of human history is one of alchemy's greatest contributions to the practice of contemporary psychological astrology.

To the extent that the influences of the outer planets remain unconscious, and therefore autonomous, the individual has no choice but to repeat and to passively perpetuate the inherited themes which reside in the collective unconscious.

The sequential discovery of the three outer planets in the eighteenth, nineteenth and twentieth centuries reflects the potential for a genuine evolution of consciousness since, whatever is discovered 'out there' in the solar system is ready to be discovered 'in here' – within each human psyche. The principles ascribed to the outer planets can no longer be projected entirely onto supernatural forces, divine or diabolic, originating from beyond the human sphere.

Now that this Pandora's box has been opened, it is no longer appropriate to remain passive victims of their influences, or to attempt to harness their powers for personal gain. It is no coincidence that the three outer planets are also associated with alienation, dissociation, delusions, addictions, compulsive behaviour, disturbing psychosomatic symptoms and mass psychoses. Jung wrote that the change of character brought about by the uprush of collective forces is amazing. "One is always inclined to lay the blame on external circumstances, but nothing could explode in us if it had not already been there."[15]

The initial task is to realise the extent to which we are subject to,

38

and therefore victims of, the collective and unconscious distortions which have us in their grip. For so long as we are unconsciously driven by the forces of the outer planets, we have no alternative but to function as conduits of mass thinking and collective ideologies (Uranus), to perpetrate an obsessive need for control and dominance (Pluto), or to remain subjected to collective delusions and suffering (Neptune), all the while believing that we are functioning as individuals.

Working alchemically, the initial task is to extract the three outer planets from their immersion in the initial chaos, or *prima materia*, of the birth chart, to bring them to individual consciousness and, in so doing, to transform our relationship to them. With an alchemical approach, the outer planets become susceptible to individual mediation.

It follows that the alchemical focus of astrological work should lie with the afflictions of the soul and to realise that, until these have been understood and attended to, genuine healing cannot occur. This is beautifully expressed by D.H. Lawrence in a poem entitled *Healing*:

"I am not a mechanism,
an assembly of various sections.
and it is not because the mechanism is working wrongly,
that I am ill.
I am ill because of wounds to the soul,
to the deep emotional self,
and the wounds to the soul take a long, long time,
only time can help
and patience,
and a certain difficult repentance
long difficult repentance,
realization of life's mistake,
and the freeing oneself
from the endless repetition
of the mistake
which mankind at large has chosen to sanctify."

The alchemical operations of the *sublimatio, calcinatio* and *solutio* provide remarkable insight into the personal relevance and creative potential of the outer planets, but they must first be repeatedly sublimated, calcinated and dissolved, if their unconscious, collective influences are to be made known and mediated by the individual. Each of these operations describes a process of personal transformation. In their initial, or lesser, manifestation, they describe "the mighty deposit of ancestral experience"[15] to which we are unconsciously subjected and by which we are unconsciously influenced, which leads to their continued blind perpetuation and projection onto the world.

The alchemists knew that it is only within the individual soul that the work can be done, that the mysterious transformations can take place, and be given back to the world. Conscious participation in the alchemical soul work gradually transforms the outer planets from their undifferentiated and yet overwhelming influences. The alchemist/ astrologer who undertakes this work is participating in the creation of consciousness. But even when the *kairos* is right, the transformations cannot be forced or imposed. The alchemist/astrologer can do no more than hold the alembic, tend the fire with gentleness and patience, with pure intentions and an attitude of prayer, in service to a source of wisdom greater than their own. Great sensitivity and respect are essential, along with a deep trust in the organic process which is occurring.

> "Change depends upon individual free will, and the development of the individual capacity to make independent choices. The 'new age' will therefore come about not as a result of a preordained pattern but as a result of the ability of humanity to realise its full potential."[16]

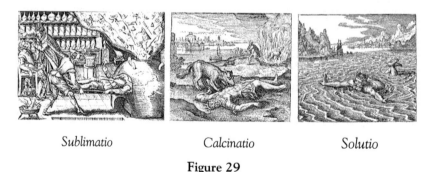

| Sublimatio | Calcinatio | Solutio |

Figure 29

In the *sublimatio*, the spirit is extracted from the *prima materia*. In the *calcinatio*, the unconscious instincts are devoured and burned in the purifying fire, and in the *solutio* they are drowned and cleansed.

The challenge is to make the right personal relationship to the outer planets, which is neither one of subservience nor of denial, and this can only be achieved with the construction of a sufficiently robust personal ego, or psychic container, which is strong enough to 'suffer the gods', as Jung so beautifully expressed it.

Saturn, as ego container, must itself be transformed in the *coagulatio* process, if it is to withstand the tensions and pressures of these operations. Without sufficient *coagulatio*, the soul has no container, no alembic, and remains unbounded, unmediated, contaminated by ancestral and historical influences, only able to function through particular mass movements which swallow up our individuality.

Endnotes

1. Baring, A. *The Dream of the Cosmos*, p.463.
2. Hillman, J. and Shamdasani, S. *The Lament of the Dead*, p.92.
3. Rudhyar, D. *The Pulse of Life*.
4. Jung, C.G. (CW13) *Alchemical Studies*, para.54.
5. See, for example, Plato, *The Republic*, Book IV.
6. Hall, Manley P. *The Secret Teachings of All Ages*, p.156.
7. Waite, E.A., *Hermetic Museum*, Vol 2, pp.142f.
8. ibid.
9. McClean, A. *A Commentary on the Rosarium Philosophorum*
10. Moore, T. *The Planets Within*, p.44.
11. Whitmont, E.C. *Return of the Goddess*, p5.
12. ibid.
13. Ebertin, R. *The Combination of Stellar Influences*. In his researches, Reinhold Ebertin discovered that there are often strong nodal links between partners and in families, those who belong to our soul group.
14. Harpur, P. *Daimonic Reality, A Field Guide to the Otherworld*, p.49.
15. Jung, C.G. CW11 *Psychology and Religion*, p.25.
16. Campion, N. *The Great Year*, p.131.

Chapter 5
Coagulatio: The Saturn Process

"Separate the earth from the fire, the subtle from the dense, gently and with great ingenuity."[1]

The Lesser Coagulatio – Finding the Lead

Coagulatio is the process of drying out anything which is volatile, liquid or gaseous, until only the substance itself remains. Emotions (water), intuitions (fire) and concepts (air) are extracted, leaving only the actual reality (earth). The *lesser coagulatio* describes the initial extraction of the lead from the chaos of the *prima materia*.

The *coagulatio* operation concretises the material, making it real and heavy, and giving it substance. The old world, bounded by Saturn, describes the circumstances of our incarnation and gives us our first shape. This equates psychologically to the development of the ego. Driven by the energy and power of its projections, the adapted ego seeks recognition, acceptance and validation in the eyes of others.

Saturn's function is to fix the boundaries, to teach us how to adapt and adjust to living in the real world, with all its physical and material limitations. Family patterns are internalized, unconsciously repeated and continue to resonate throughout our lives.

Figure 30
The Saturn key

Like Chronos, terrified of being usurped, the parents may unconsciously repeat their own ancestral inheritance and swallow the life force and unique potential of their children. The archetype of the dark father, and of the dark mother who supports him, is driven by fear, control and repression.

Like the mythic Chiron, rejected son of Chronos/Saturn, our souls may be neither recognised nor welcomed by the community into which we have been born. Finding ourselves in an alien world, we may grow up feeling judged, isolated and fearful, and blame ourselves for our presumed inadequacies and vulnerability. As we adapt to our environment, our innate potential, longings and creative gifts may remain undeveloped. Our faith in the world is shattered and we feel the pain of existence.

Chiron describes the suffering of a soul which has not yet recognised the parental and ancestral origins of its pain. The hero is constellated and we become determined, at all costs, to conceal our feelings of guilt or shame.

Saturn transits threaten the ego's carefully constructed ruling principles of consciousness, represented in alchemy by the old king and queen. They can be interpreted as emotional turning points, opportunities to realise and confront the limitations of our socially constructed identity, of previous dependencies and old ways of being. If we are to discover the solid rock of our own existence, our identification with the external world has to die.

Coagulatio processes often make themselves known when, in spite of what may appear to be relatively successful lives, relationships, social networks and careers, we begin to feel unfulfilled and disappointed – is this all there is? As the call from our deeper, unknown selves becomes more pressing, so our feeling of alienation from ourselves increases.

Fearful of the call, it is not unusual to attempt to strengthen our defences by retrenching, regressing and retreating into former patterns of identity which may have long outlived their usefulness but which, by virtue of their familiarity, appear to offer safety and containment. Originally constructed to keep us safe, the ego's defences are then further crystallised and calcified, and we become increasingly fearful, rigid, judgemental and paranoid.

> "Bound in by the walls of childhood; the father and mother stand as threshold guardians, and the timorous soul, fearful of some punishment, fails to make the passage through the door and come to birth in the world without."[2]

The Death of the Old King and Queen
The alchemists knew that the first parents, the old king and queen, must die.

> "The previously dominant and domineering conscious mind has outlived its usefulness and must be broken down, but its loss is fraught

with fear and a profound sense of grief for what once was. This is the price of becoming real."[3]

Figure 31
The ruling principle of consciousness is devoured by the instincts

Numerous alchemical images show the king or the Sun, symbols of the ruling principle of consciousness, being devoured by the instincts, by nature, often in the form of the green lion. In this image the body of the lion contains the seven planets, representing their instinctual, spontaneous and dynamic energies, which seek renewed creative expression. We can no longer protect ourselves from the life force which seeks to penetrate the bars of the cage we have so carefully constructed for ourselves. Saturn transits can be understood as a call to grow beyond the old structures which originally represented safety and security but which no longer serve us. It is time for our fragile, hard won, ego-constructed identity to be mortified in order for a new centre to emerge.

Confrontation with the Shadow
The alchemical stages of the *nigredo*, the *mortificatio* and the *putrefactio* correspond psychologically to the encounter with the shadow, an inevitable by-product of ego development.

Identified by Jung as the *personal unconscious*, the shadow holds memories of fear, shame, guilt, anxiety and unacknowledged rage, which have their origin in early traumatic experiences. But the shadow also harbours innate but unrealised abilities and strengths which have not been recognised or nurtured by our family or culture, or which have been judged or repressed, and which we have therefore lacked the confidence to develop.

In the *coagulatio* processes, the *prima materia*, the original chaos, is suffocated in the alembic. The false self is dying, and we are faced with our shadow, with all our customary evasions, escapes, denials and projections. We can no longer continue to blame everyone else for our circumstances. We are growing up and, one way or another, we are being asked to face the reality.

It is time for the fantasies to be stripped away and rendered down, until we are left with what we actually are. The *coagulatio* process is identified with death, and many people undergoing a Saturn transit feel, literally, as if they are dying, but this can usually be interpreted symbolically: that they are dying to their old selves, to old life chapters, outgrown identifications and childish dependencies.

For people who are well attuned to the demands of Saturn, already familiar with the earth principle and used to living in the real world, the process of *coagulatio* can be welcomed. They have developed the resilience to endure and survive, even when the foundations of their lives seem to have been reduced to dust and ashes. They know that tangible, material achievements demand commitment, time and effort, and bring their own rewards.

The uncoagulated spirit is free and autonomous, able to entertain any fantasies and beliefs without consequence. For people with a predominance of planets in the fire signs, the *coagulatio* can be extremely painful. The extraction of fire causes a loss of meaning, a crisis of the spirit. No longer inspired or enthused, they feel heavy, bogged down, bored, exhausted, disillusioned or cynical. The bigger picture is lost, the sense of unlimited potential recedes, and they begin to feel that time is running out.

For people with a predominance of planets in the air signs, there is a loss of perspective, of their customary detachment and objectivity, of the comfort of intellectual abstraction. They can feel trapped, no longer able to think themselves through what feel like painful periods of stasis or incarceration.

As the moisture is extracted from the material in the flask, the old dependencies are dried up. For people with a predominance of planets in the water signs, Saturn transits impose periods of separation and isolation. There may be an obvious cause, such as a betrayal or abandonment, a failed marriage or career, the loss of home, health or financial security. The previous structures which have represented emotional and material support collapse and only the cold reality remains.

Nigredo

The word *nigredo* means blackness – symbolised in alchemical imagery by the raven. The alchemist would fall into a 'blackness blacker than black', which he saw reflected in the blackening of the matter in the alchemical retort. And yet, the alchemical texts frequently comment that 'when you see your matter going black, rejoice: for that is the beginning of the work'.

Figure 32
Symbols of the *nigredo*

In other words, the conscious endurance of darkness eventually leads to renewal and to the birth of a radically different kind of authority, less rigid and more flexible, related and magnanimous, a transformed expression of Saturn.

Understanding the transits of Saturn in terms of the *coagulatio* provides an alchemical context for those times when we feel isolated and melancholy. The *coagulatio* has its place and needs to be honoured, and we can often sense that Saturn transits are meaningful on a level we are not yet able to understand. It may be time to come to terms with the echoes of the past, to remember old sorrows, to feel our melancholy and to complete a mourning or grieving process which could not be done before. There may be more salt to be mined, more meaning to be discovered.

The imagery of the *coagulatio* is entombment, being turned to stone, but each time we emerge from a Saturn transit, we have added another layer of experience, and the lead is gradually turning into gold.

Figure 33 illustrates the isolation of the *nigredo* state. The alchemist sits and meditates in a bleak desert landscape. The black crow or raven, symbol of death, is his only companion. But all things celestial and divine are still present. The *nigredo* is overseen by the seven planets and by the winged figures of soul and spirit. The winds blowing in the top corners signify that, in spite of the stillness, isolation and waiting, this is, in fact, a time of change.

Figure 33
The *nigredo*

47

Figure 34 shows a further development of the *nigredo* process: the alchemist has now become skeletal, no more than skin and bone (both ruled by Saturn), and the black crow sits on his body. The immortal spirit and soul have been exhaled, but sugnificantly, they still remain within the contained space of the alembic. The purpose of the *coagulatio*, then, is to confront our mortality, to discover what supports us when everything else has been taken away. However desolate this image may

Figure 34
The death of the old king, as *spiritus* and *anima* are exhaled

be, once again the breath of the winds clearly indicates that this is a time of change, attended by the Sun and Moon and the five planets; it is a meaningful, contained and necessary process.

Putrefactio and Mortificatio

The *mortificatio* is felt as a deep melancholy, a darkness of the mind, an affliction of the soul. Images of darkness, defeat, torture, dismemberment, death and rotting are found throughout the alchemical texts.

Figure 35
putrefactio

Psychologically, the *mortificatio* signifies that the corpse, the old ego identity, has died, is rotting in the *putrefactio* and must be properly buried. It is time to put the past to rest by grieving, mourning and burying it.[4]

> "Through depression we enter depths and in depths find soul. It moistens the dry soul, and dries the wet, it brings refuge, limitations, focus, gravity, weight and humble powerlessness. It reminds us of death. The true revolution begins in the individual who can be true to his own depression."[5]

The experience of the *nigredo* is beautifully described by T.S. Eliot in his poem East Coker:

> "I said to my soul, be still, and wait without hope
> For hope would be hope for the wrong thing; wait without love
> For love would be love for the wrong thing; there is yet faith
> But the faith and the love and the hope are all in the waiting.
> Wait without thought, for you are not ready for thought:
> So the darkness shall be the light, and the stillness the dancing."

The Greater Coagulatio

The death and resurrection of the king is a theme often explored by the alchemists, and can be found in the *Splendor Solis*, the *Rosarium* and many other texts. The following images are from the *Pretiosa Margarita*

(Pearl of Great Price), by Janus Lacinius (Leipzig edition, 1714).

The series begins with the old king, or Saturn/ Chronos, on his throne, attended by the six remaining planets, each clothed in the relevant planetary colours. As this illustration shows, the initial task of the planets is to serve Saturn and, as agents of the *coagulatio*, they have their own parts to play in the building of our ego identity.

In the following illustrations, Mercury, as instigator of the transformation, kills the king and removes his heart, before laying him in a coffin. This is followed by the *nigredo*, *mortificatio* and *putrefactio*, a long period of waiting and praying and endurance, during which the bones of the dead king are dismembered and rearranged.

 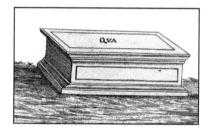

The Reborn King

Eventually the new king is born, now radically transformed. In the *greater coagulatio*, very different values emerge from the depths of the soul of the reborn king. There are now only five external planets, a graphic representation of the fact that, in the process of the death and rebirth of the king, the solar and lunar principles have become united in the mystical marriage of opposites.

The new king holds out his hand to the planetary deities in a gesture of relationship and protective authority. The planets themselves are now crowned, signifying that they too have been transformed. Initially defined and inhibited by the collective values of the old king, their essential, personal, life affirming qualities are now released, freed for renewed creative expression.

The inclusion of the feminine principle, and acceptance of our mortality leads to the greater *coagulatio*, a procedure which brings consciousness into a living, functioning, embodied, personal reality. New life is breathed into the material residue and the heavenly substances of the planets are no longer hidden, but revealed, as described in the following alchemical recipe:

"Venus is brought to life again by the addition of honey, symbolising sweetness, the pleasure of the senses and the joy of life, including the danger of worldly entanglements. Jupiter is strengthened by the addition of celandine, or chelidonia, symbolising the beauty of wholeness, and rosemary, as the 'dew of the sea', describes the grace which drips from the Moon. Mercury is represented by the androgenous mercurialis plant, symbolising sexual libido, stimulating the desires of Mars and Venus, and the red lily symbolises the heart's blood which will reunite the separated soul/spirit with the body."[6]

The Sun

No longer driven by immature arrogance and naïve hubris, the Sun has completed its full cycle, has died at the midnight point, where opposites meet, and has been reborn, now united with the Moon. Spirit has been given substance, brought down to earth, anchored and grounded in matter. The transformed Sun has been initiated into adulthood with a new centre of gravity. Mature solar consciousness is generative, creative and empowering of the self and others. Revitalised, it emerges with a wider vision of the whole, and submits to its role as a channel through which the flow of life can be released into the world.

Under the rulership of the old king and queen, the healthy and joyful expression of the Moon and Venus, is a rarity. More often than not, the feminine planets are severely undervalued, distorted and consigned to the individual and collective shadows.

The Moon

The Moon is associated with nature, matter and mother, with everything which feeds, nourishes and protects us. As the principle of embodiment, it is therefore an essential aspect of the *coagulatio*. But in our culture it is not unusual to treat the body as the enemy. Valid and normal physical and emotional needs are habitually denied, starved, judged or ignored altogether. Alternatively, they are overindulged without measure. Feelings of great hunger, emotional deprivation, eating disorders and spacial disorientation can be understood symbolically as a fear, or rejection, of the *coagulatio*, a refusal to accept or embrace our incarnation.

But the body and the instincts cannot be left out of the *coagulatio*. Physical symptoms emerging during Saturn transits often concern the skeletal structure, skin, teeth, knees and backs, rheumatism or arthritis, reminding us of the temporal nature and limitations of the physical body. Accompanying periods of illness or depression may well serve the *coagulatio*, insofar as they promote a withdrawal from the world, a time for contemplation.

When allied to the transformed Saturn, we learn how to feed and care appropriately for the Moon in our birth charts, with patience, compassion and acceptance.

Venus

In many spiritual traditions it is believed that the incarnation of the soul is governed by desire and Venus is, of course, the planet of desire. Desire promotes *coagulatio* but has long been associated with the sins of the flesh, as in the lascivious Pan aspect of Saturn, with his horns and hooves. *Coagulatio* is explicitly associated with evil and with Saturn as a malefic principle, so it is no wonder that so many people are afraid of their desires. And yet, if we are to experience the joy of being alive, we need to seek, cultivate and act on our desires, according to the natal position of Venus in our charts.

Mercury

Saturn and Mercury are gate keepers, ruling thresholds and boundaries. As Saturn transforms, so our polarisations and rigid defences soften. A fully coagulated Mercury, as *mercurius senex*, is the product of the marriage of opposites. Knowing that the truth is fundamentally paradoxical, *mercurius senex* is able to walk between the worlds and mediate between different realities and different truths. Released from the immature fear of being wrong or being found out, which leads to evasion and deceit, Mercury's perceptions gain weight and perspective, and at last we find our own voice.

Mars

In service to the fear and paranoia of the old king, Mars turns inwards, against itself, and the survival instinct is blocked. Bloodless, passive and cowardly, an uncoagulated Mars is powerless and impotent, inviting victimisation. As Saturn transforms, Mars is released for effective creative expression in service to the transformed king. Newly-honed and focused, there no longer anything to fear. As the source of our personal potency and strength, we discover our courage and willpower, the ability to achieve our goals, and to defend ourselves and others.

Jupiter

In Greek and Roman mythology it was Zeus/Jupiter who released his siblings, the other planets, after they had been swallowed by Chronos/Saturn. The old, fearful, titan king had to die and be replaced by the new Olympian order, led by Zeus. Stepping into his new authority, a fully coagulated Jupiter has become steadied and more realistic. Over-optimism, arrogance and excess are replaced by appreciation and gratitude. Jupiter's enthusiasm, generosity and sense of abundance are extended for the benefit of the wider community.

Saturn

As Saturn transforms, the revitalised planets become the channels through which the flow of life can be released into the world. Fully embodied, the new ruling principle of consciousness (Sun) is instinctive (Moon), passionate (Venus), inclusive (Mercury), vigorous (Mars) and generous (Jupiter). In his turn, Saturn is released to *bend the knee* in the service of spirit, one of the most profound meanings of the sign of Capricorn.

Working with the *Coagulatio*

Coagulatio themes are constellated every six or seven years, when Saturn makes a hard aspect to its natal position, and whenever Saturn transits over a planet, the nodal axis or one of the angles in the birth chart. The Saturn returns, around the ages of 29 and 59, represent the completion of entire life chapters.

Feelings of paralysis, exhaustion and illness can be a feature of the *coagulatio*, but periods of retreat, isolation and contemplation are often necessary for the soul. Old regrets and sadnesses re-emerge, memories of past abandonments, the loss or death of loved ones, and opportunities lost. The time has come to put them to rest by grieving, mourning and burying them. Courage, endurance and patience are called for during the long period of lying, as if dead, in the sarcophagus. It is time to honour the darkness and to stay steady.

During the Saturn returns, it is time to take stock, to reassess past experiences and decisions made. It may be appropriate to reap the rewards of past achievements, or to recognise that old goals for status, recognition and acceptance may no longer be so relevant or meaningful to us. Often there are decisions to be made, upon which a great deal appears to hang. Either way, the change has to come from within and it can seem that, on a deep, inner level, we are being asked to choose whether to live or die.

Janet was forty-one years old, at the time of her second Saturn opposition. The focus of our our initial sessions was on her disappointment and frustration that she had not achieved her ambition to become a successful and recognised writer, and her fear that time was running out. It transpired that her father had died an exact Saturn cycle earlier, when she was thirteen years old. Janet remembered how he had supported and encouraged her early promise as a writer, and how she had lost her self-belief after his death. With Saturn transiting through her twelfth house, it was time to recognise how much grief and sadness she still carried, to come to terms with her loss, and to complete her mourning for him, and for the child she still was at the time. In a year or so, Saturn would transit over her Ascendant, with all its promise for new beginnings. It would soon be time for Janet to find the courage to step out into the world with renewed confidence, personal authority and a new loyalty to herself and to her goals.

Victoria was approaching her second Saturn return when her husband of many years asked for a divorce. She had identified herself almost entirely as a wife and mother, and devoted her life to being a home maker and raising her daughters. Although her marriage had not been happy for some time, it nevertheless represented safety, financial security and social standing. She felt deeply betrayed, particularly by old, married friends who increasingly distanced themselves from her. Forced to sell the family home, she moved to an isolated area in the country to be near one of her daughters. But her daughter was offered a job abroad and, knowing nobody in the area, she found herself utterly alone, during two extremely harsh winters. Snowed in for long periods, Victoria had never felt colder, and her daily ritual was in graphic homage to Saturn, as she

55

brought in the coal and cleared out the ashes in an effort to keep warm during the long dark nights.

During this long period, Victoria found the courage to endure, to stay steady, and to honour the darkness, and she began, at last, to rediscover herself. Gradually, she started to paint again, something she had not done since her marriage, and decided to embark on a homoeopathic training course, a subject which had always interested her. This was one of the most difficult and challenging things she had ever done, but she persevered and qualified as a practitioner at the age of 64, when Saturn transited her North Node in Capricorn. Although she had not consciously chosen this path, she felt that she was at last coming into her own, began to embrace her newfound freedom and autonomy and found a professional outlet in which she could continue to care for others, but now as a healer and woman of age and wisdom.

Conversely, **Emma** was a fifty-eight-year-old woman with natal Saturn on her Midheaven in Sagittarius. A career woman all her life, she had had her own successful company for many years, organising international conferences. But she was losing enthusiasm for her job, and lacked the energy, and even the desire, to put in the effort required to make the necessary changes which would take her business forward. Emma was having problems with her back, and was consumed by feelings of paralysis, hesitation and doubt.

Astrologically, she was in transition from the second to the third Saturn cycle, and in the long process of adjusting to a significant new chapter in her life. As we explored the themes of the *coagulatio* together, Emma recognised that her old goals for professional status and recognition were no longer relevant or meaningful to her. During our last session she was beginning to think about taking up riding again, a great joy which she had not had time for while running her business, and she was even thinking about opening a refuge for retired horses.

Gradually, as the Saturn transits pass, we feel ready to step back out into the world again, emerging with a new internal centre of gravity and a newfound loyalty to ourselves. We have mourned for the child and become adult, able to protect, nurture and support the child within. We may feel older and more tired, but we have a new sense of authority, confidence and self-acceptance. We have learned to trust and be true to our own values, and no longer need to hide from ourselves or from others.

The Outer Planets

The outer planets must also, of course, be included in the astrological *opus*, and the following three chapters explore the alchemical transformations of Uranus, Neptune and Pluto, as we awaken to our soul's purpose.

Endnotes

1. *The Emerald Tablet*, see Appendix I: para.7.
2. Campbell, J. *The Hero with a Thousand Faces*, p.62.
3. Stein, M. *In Midlife*, p.41.
4. ibid pp.27-34.
5. Hillman, J. *Re-Visioning Psychology*, pp.98-9.
6. Jung, C.G. (CW14) *Mysterium Coniunctionis*, para.704.

Chapter 6
Sublimatio: The Uranus Process

"It ascends from the earth to heaven, and descends again to the earth, and receives the power of the above and the below. Thus you will have the glory of the whole world. Therefore all darkness will flee from you."[1]

The Transformation of the Outer Planets

In the initial process of *separatio*, unity is divided into polarity, positive and negative, personified in alchemy by the many images of the king and queen, *sol* and *luna*. At the level of three, the mysterious realm of the soul is revealed, illustrated throughout the alchemical literature as the dragon or serpent mercurius. And the fourfold nature of matter describes the essential physical and psychological orientation of each person's personality and character. In the *coagulatio*, or Saturn process, a strong and flexible alembic is created, without which the incarnation of the spirit and soul cannot proceed.

The scene is now set for work to begin on the three parts of the soul, the archetypal sources of knowledge, wisdom and compassion. Represented astrologically by Uranus, Pluto and Neptune, they must be identified and transformed separately in the alchemical retort, or birth chart.

Each alchemical operation has two major stages, a lesser and a greater. In the first stage the individual is unknowingly used by, and subjected to the inherited residues of the personal and collective unconscious, and has no alternative but to continue to perpetrate, and passively suffer from their influences. The second stage describes the radical metamorphoses which occur as the outer planets are released from their historical contamination and returned, through individual effort, to their archetypal values.

Sublimatio

The term 'sublimatio' derives from the Latin **sublimis**, meaning 'high', or 'to raise or lift', to 'elevate into a higher form by an ascent'. For the

58

alchemists, the *sublimatio* process involved heating the material in the flask until it volatised and evaporated, turning into a gas. The extracted *essence* of the material would ascend to the upper, cooler region of the vessel and there condense into a dew. The process of distillation is similar, the extraction of the essential nature of a thing in a concentrated, purified form.

In alchemical imagery, flying birds normally symbolise the spirited part of the soul, and in Figure 36, repeated sublimations and distillations are taking place within the alembic. As the bird of the *sublimatio* flies upwards and downwards, the four elements at the base of the flask become agitated as more and more of the spirit is extracted. Gradually, the turmoil of the four elements is resolved, until only the distilled essence itself remains at the base of the flask, above which a star appears.

Figure 36
Repeated sublimations and distillations

Sulphur: The Spirited part of the Soul

"Nature, whose power is in her obedience to the Will of God, ordained from the very beginning that the four elements should incessantly act on one another, so, in obedience to her behest, **fire began to act on air, and *produced Sulphur*;** air acted on water and produced *Mercury*; water, by its action on earth, produced *Salt*. Earth, alone, having nothing to act upon, did not produce anything, but became the nurse, or womb, of these three Principles.[2]

Sulphur relates to the spirited part of the soul, a combination of the positive, masculine, elements of air and fire, intellect and intuition,

59

represented astrologically by Uranus. In the *sublimatio*, the ideas and concepts of air are fueled by the vision and revelation of fire.

The spirited part of the soul is remote, exalted, transcendant and eternal. Spirit releases us from the dense confines and restrictions of material existence, from ordinary fallible human suffering, and from the physical and emotional compulsions which drive us from within.

Uranus operates on a non-biological level. Its motivation is to achieve intellectual detachment. It represents the ability to 'get above' a concrete problem by extracting its symbolic or *essential* meaning and seeing it objectively. Just to find suitable words or concepts can be enough to gain perspective and release ourselves from the grip of emotional turmoil and confusion. Myths, stories, symbols and analogies are all examples of *sublimatio*, revealing the essential essence of the universal patterns which live through us. It is tempting to assume, however, that abstractions have the highest value, and that once something has been theoretically evaluated, the goal has been achieved.

The discovery of Uranus destroyed at a stroke the old world bounded by Saturn, creating a kind of intellectual vertigo, a new faith in science and in unlimited progress. The old order was challenged by a completely new kind of radical, secular thinking. The natural world lost its sacred, living attributes and, with the emergence of scientific materialism, modern science came into its own. Scientists were finally freed to penetrate the structure of matter without any danger of tampering with the divine, or consideration of the consequences of doing so.

Despite its radical secularization, the quest to improve upon nature is now stronger than ever, crystallized around the current theologies of materialism, positivism and infinite progress. More than ever, we are collectively gripped by the alchemical ideal, although it is now driven by the desire to harness, control and dominate nature in the interests of scientific, industrial, medical and horticultural advancement. Uranus describes the creative spark which leads to cultural and technological breakthroughs, sudden revelation, enlightenment, intellectual and spiritual awakening, and the enhancement of human autonomy. Named after the distant god of the starry heavens, Uranus has increasingly come to be associated with the myth of Prometheus, with the appropriation by mankind of powers which were once the preserve of the gods.

In a profoundly alchemical passage, Jung wrote that through the coming into being of the conscious self-reflective mind, mankind has become "indispensable for the completion of creation, a second creator of the world, who alone has given to the world its objective existence."[3]

The Lesser Sublimatio

Uranus in the birth chart gives us detachment and perspective, access to intuitive flashes of knowledge or revelations which appear to come from beyond our conscious awareness. As a collective force, it engenders a conviction of absolute truth and entitlement. Everyone born within a particular seven year period will be caught up in a collective vision which seeks liberation from the traditional meaning of the sign it falls into. Uranus is responsible for genuine insight and innovation, but there is often a fanatical and brutal edge to this ideology and, if the Uranian vision remains collective, we may become possessed by, and unconsciously continue to perpetuate, the tyranny of mass thinking.

Uranus rules both genius and insanity and, until we have found ourselves in the crowd we will continue to function as unconscious conduits of any number of intellectual straightjackets. Ordinary human concerns, feelings and values are ignored or sacrificed to the spirit of the time. Contemptuous of the inability of 'ordinary mortals' to see the wider view, the Uranian vision may be worn as a badge of honour, and used to demonstrate spiritual, intellectual or moral superiority.

In Figure 37, the spirit escapes from its worldly confinements and ascends the planetary ladder, coming to rest in eternity.

Severed from a meaningful connection with nature and the body, the natural world all too easily becomes the enemy to be mastered, manipulated and controlled. The relative freedom and perspective of the sublimated state is an important achievement, but it can be disastrous to be stuck in the sky. Objectivity can be a source of consciousness,

Figure 37
The alchemical steps from base matter to pure spirit

61

but in its extreme expression it can become an autonomous process of dissociation, a cause of mental illness.

The higher we go the grander and more comprehensive is our perspective, but also the more remote we become from actual life and the less able we will be to have an effect on what we perceive.

Each alchemical operation, taken to extremes, has its own particular pathology and, as Jung wrote: "The intellect in supreme position is demonic. If it is tacitly recognised as the supreme power it will not be noticed how demonic it is. It can become the uncontested dominant of one's psychic life."[4] Blinded by the brilliance of unprecedented scientific and technological discoveries, it is all too easy to become possessed by the power drive of the unconscious Uranian shadow.

The alchemists knew that the *sublimatio* was accompanied by a distinct whiff of sulphur, or brimstone, a well known characteristic of hell. An inflamable element, its vapours stink and blacken most metals. Astrology is itself associated with the Uranian principle and is a perfect example of the *sublimatio* process. The construction of a horoscope, or indeed of any map, table or system, enables us to stand outside it, and in the process to gain detachment, objectivity and perspective. It gives us a breathing space; we can explore ourselves in projection and through that process gain insight.

Astrological client work is a deliberate act of sublimation, providing clients with an external standpoint which enables them, often for the very first time, to see their lives reflected within the scheme of the universe. What have often, until then, been experienced as a relatively chaotic and jumbled collection of feelings and events can, even in a single session, bring a sense of perspective, order and reassurance. An astrological viewpoint places our individual experiences within a universal context, enables us to gain significant insight into our inner worlds and become reflective spectators of our lives.

There is great beauty in the symbolic structure of an astrological chart, but fascinating intellectual models can all too easily become abstractions, techniques or diagnoses used to avoid or explain away painful human emotions, times of despair, loss or mourning. There is a fine line to tread, since the undoubted value of the *sublimatio* process, and one of astrology's greatest gifts, is its ability to provide a wider, more universal context, to help us rise above an actual situation and see it from a symbolic perspective. But it can all too easily become a technique used to help us dissociate from, or explain away, our feelings.

In themselves, intellectual or academic insights are useless unless they are grounded, followed through, applied in practice. Dreams, images and visions that refer to upward movement – ascent, flying, heights, or the attainment of spiritual insight – can indicate that the psyche is undergoing a process of *sublimatio* and almost always indicates the need for a down-going. Equally, bird phobias or a fear of flying may symbolise a resistance to the *sublimatio*.

The Greater Sublimatio
Severed from its connection with soul and body, the ultimate *sublimatio* of the spirit is physical death. It is clear from the alchemical texts and illustrations that the ascent alone does not constitute the entire process of *sublimatio*. For the alchemists the task was to '*sublimate the body and coagulate the spirit*'. As the alchemical images show, both upward and downward movement are of equal importance.

Intellectual, academic or spiritual insights are of immense value, but they are not the goal of the *opus*. They need to be weighed by the human heart and, if they are found to be of value, given back to the world. This is why the alembic – the birth chart – must be sealed, so that the sublimated essence, the spiritual aspect of the soul, can condense into a dew and return to the world.

> "Just as the ascending birds represent sublimatio and translation from the temporal to the eternal, so descending birds represent contents from the archetypal world that are incarnating by breaking into the personal ego realm."[5]

Provided that the alembic remains sealed, in other words, provided that Uranus remains capable of transformation, the body and soul continue to call us backwards and downwards to engage with the personal and specific circumstances of our lives. In due course, after many repeated experiences of *sublimatio*, a dew forms at the top of the sealed alembic and begins to descend upon, and reanimate, the previously despised, abandoned material below. This is graphically illustrated in the many alchemical images of the eagle of spirit flying upwards, rising like a phoenix but, for so long as we are incarnate, chained to the toad of matter, nature and the body.

The dew symbolises the moisture, the healing grace which restores life to the intellectual wasteland. The moisture corresponds to the recovery of feeling after succumbing to the deadly, barren state of intellectual abstraction, like Faust's before his encounter with Mephistopheles. The *greater sublimatio* can only be achieved by the individual. In other words, the insights gained must be personalised, made real and grounded in life.

In Figure 38, *mercurius*, in the form of a serpent, holds the opposites together, keeping the connection between the spiritual and material parts of the soul. As always, *mercurius* guides the processes of separation and reunion. The united Sun and Moon in the centre indicate that the *greater sublimatio* is an essential aspect of the *mystical marriage*. The Moon is the source of dew, the sap of the water of life, the healing grace which reconnects the separated fragments of our psyches.

Figure 38
The upward and downward movement of the *greater sublimatio*

Ultimately, then, as the spirited part of the soul, Uranus is transformed by the descent of the dew. In the birth chart it comes to represent the seat of true knowledge tempered by morality. It is expressed as a kind of detached compassion and empathy, and the ability to rise above the particulars to universal principles, without losing touch with the heart. Problems are resolved and questions answered from an inclusive and loving perspective, as so beautifully expressed in Portia's speech in the *Merchant of Venice*, Act 4, Scene 1:

"The quality of mercy is not strain'd,
It droppeth as the gentle rain from heaven
Upon the place beneath: it is twice blest;

It blesseth him that gives and him that takes:
'Tis mightiest in the mightiest: it becomes
The throned monarch better than his crown;
His sceptre shows the force of temporal power,
The attribute to awe and majesty,
Wherein doth sit the dread and fear of kings;
But mercy is above this sceptred sway;
It is enthroned in the hearts of kings,
It is an attribute to God himself;
And earthly power doth then show likest God's
When mercy seasons justice."

Figure 39
The self-sacrifice of the pelican

A transformed Uranus involves a voluntary return to human values and to the world, in the knowledge that the gift of individual insight, when grounded in the heart, becomes a permanent addition to the growth of collective consciousness.

In the *greater sublimatio*, the alchemical pelican bites into its own breast, opens its heart and lets out its life blood to nurture and fertilise the earth, enabling new life to grow. Sublimated souls open their heart's blood for the redemption of the earth and compassion becomes part of the process of creation.

Sublimatio: Uranus and the story of Faust

"For what shall it profit a man, if he shall gain the whole world, and lose his own soul?"[6]

The legend of Faust is based on the life of the fifteenth century German alchemist and astrologer. The most famous literary works on the Faust theme are Christopher Marlowe's *The Tragical History of Doctor Faustus* and Johann Wolfgang von Goethe's *Faust*. There are many variations on the Faustian theme in theatre, music, film, poetry and literature, but in all cases alchemy appears to be the common thread. Today, the term

65

'Faustian' is used to describe powerful people who betray their principles and values in order to achieve their goals for super-human knowledge and power.

With remarkable prescience, Goethe wrote his poem 'Prometheus' at the age of twenty five, seven years before the discovery of Uranus in 1781. It was a vision of human progress and autonomy, of the freedom of the individual to challenge the omnipotence of the gods by stealing the divine fire, a vision he later extended in his play, Faust.[8]

Faust has also been described as a prophetic tale about the destiny of western civilisation, written as Europe began its transformation from a religious to a secular society. It tells of the tragic human consequences of cutting ourselves off from, and attempting to control, the natural world, and of appropriating more power than we can handle. As in the case of Faust, the conclusion remains hanging in the balance.

Figure 40
Faust in his study

> "We are Faust. We have made a bargain with the devil for enormous power over the earth. We have committed crimes against nature and humanity for the sake of more land, more energy, more destructive capacity."[7]

The story of Faust explores his pursuit of unnatural values in a godless age, in the sense that they are cut off from, and even hostile towards, nature. Faust's achievements, such as they were, are artificial, entirely man made, and driven by his greed for superhuman power.

But Goethe's play can also be understood as an alchemical allegory describing the tragic consequences of Faust's failed attempts to achieve a genuine *coniunctio* by uniting in love with the feminine principle. Confronted with the conflict between love and power, Faust consistently chooses power, and all his attempted unions end in failure and death, causing him grief and increasing guilt.

Working with the Sublimatio

Transits of the outer planets may only cover an arc of their full cycles during a lifetime. But their transits over a planet, angle or the nodal axis can last for several years and, as our insights and understanding of their deeper levels of meaning grows, they begin to find transformed expression in our lives. The transits of the outer planets therefore represent work in progress, inherited from our ancestors and bequeathed to our descendants. They describe the potential for the evolution of consciousness of the *anima mundi*, the collective soul of our species, and the role which each individual has to play in this metamorphosis.

In the case of Uranus, more and more people are living to experience its complete 84-year cycle. Uranus spends approximately seven years in each sign, describing how and where, according to its house, everybody born within that period has access to radical new insights and ways of thinking, which are collective pattern breakers.

Like all the alchemical procedures, *sublimatio* processes can only proceed under the right astrological conditions. They must wait for the *kairos*, and are normally activated when Uranus transits over a planet or angle in the birth chart, or the nodal axis, or in aspect to its natal position, most noticeably at the squares (around the ages of twenty-one and sixty-three) and the opposition (around the age of forty-two).

Uranus, as the principle of detachment, acts as the awakener, and people with an emphasis of planets in fire and air signs may welcome the sudden revelations or realisations which arrive with its transits. They often herald a breakthrough in understanding, new perspectives, the ability to see things differently, from a more abstract, liberated viewpoint, which can lead to a radical severing of old patterns and assumptions.

Sublimatio brings insight, but many people don't really want to change. People with an emphasis of planets in the elements of earth and water or in the fixed signs may resist this call of the spirit. Habitual emotional and physical attachments may be unexpectedly or suddenly broken, which can be shocking, and cause painful feelings of loss and disorientation. It can be difficult to let go, but so much of which we think is concretely true and real turns out, in fact, to have a symbolic core.

During transits of Uranus, it can be helpful to explore what our attachments actually symbolise for us: what do they stand for? For this spiritual aspect of the soul desires not the thing itself but what it symbolises, in the imagination.

Money, for example, represents value, worth, security, freedom, choice and, in our culture, success and power. Ultimately, these are symbolic values which become attached to the acquisition of physical wealth. Equally, relationships may symbolise comfort, acceptance, companionship, physical closeness and reassurance that we are likeable or lovable, all values which become attached to the relationship itself, which is why it can be so devastating when relationships break up. Children are symbols of our creativity and urge for immortality, but there are many other avenues for creative expression. Uranus lifts us out of our concrete attachments, enabling us to understand their underlying symbolism. The desires of the soul are no longer lost in materialism.

But Uranus in the chart also describes how and where we are cut off from, or tend to 'rise above' our feelings and ordinary human concerns, adopting ideologies and intellectual justifications which mask our alienation. Uranus transits often carry an irresistible compulsion to sever old ties and gain release from old patterns. But the clarity and conviction which drives the compulsion to make radical changes is often projected onto external circumstances and may interfere with, or obscure the potential for, a more integrated understanding of the deeper purpose of this call to spirit.

As a general rule, for example, the Uranus in Libra generation brings an enlightened, more liberated approach to relationships. They tend to adhere to the highest values of truth, honesty and friendship, a position which can be sustained only for as long as they remain objective and emotionally detached. With this placement, there is a tendency to break off from any relationships which threaten to become too close, or which do not conform to their intellectual ideals. The Uranus in Scorpio generation instinctively avoids any inherited emotional swamplands, believing that it is possible to transcend them. But real change or liberation from past patterns can only truly come with compassionate understanding, symbolised by the descent of the alchemical dew. The Uranus in Sagittarius generation seeks to transcend inherited cultural and religious allegiances. In the process they can become disorientated and particularly vulnerable to being caught up in cults, grooming or radicalisation. For the Uranus in Capricorn generation, the old cultural containers have lost their historical context and meaning. As traditional loyalties and allegiances disappear, they are replaced by periods of widespread confusion. This generation is prone to becoming 'stuck in the sky', displaced, anxious and alienated from their bodies and from the natural world. But as the *sublimatio* processes unfold and their personal relationship to Uranus transforms, the gift of this generation is to come back to earth and to start to build the new structures for the future.

When I first met **Martin**, he was in the grip of his Uranus opposition. A brilliant mathematician, he was working for a major financial investment company in London, for whom he had devised a unique and extremely successful algorithm. But Martin felt disdain towards his work colleagues, who seemed unable to recognise or appreciate his remarkable talent. He also felt that his spirit was dying inside the constraints and limitations of his role in the company.

Martin left his job and started up his own enterprise, which was initially very successful. But he became increasingly irritated that so many potential clients did not understand his thinking, and he retreated, like Ouronos, the sky god, further and further into his mind. He became increasingly isolated, gradually alienating his peers and losing touch with his family and friends. Eventually, as he continued to pursue his vision, his marriage broke up and after a while he no longer saw his children.

Martin had always felt like an outsider and, similar to many contemporary birth charts, his chart contained the maverick Uranus/ Chiron opposition. His actions and behaviour exacerbated his feelings of alienation, and he failed to genuinely engage with the clients he needed if he was to achieve what he believed was his potential for great wealth and recognition. But the origin and root cause of the Uranus/Chiron opposition usually lies with the parents or ancestors, and recognising that this is an inherited pattern can generate new insight, understanding and forgiveness.

Linda has a predominantly fixed chart with Mercury, Sun, Mars and Saturn in Aquarius. Like so many Aquarians, she is idealistic, principled, fair, honest and loyal. She also has extremely fixed opinions and beliefs and, as a corporate lawyer, her clarity was greatly valued in her profession.

She first consulted me when Uranus was transiting her Ascendant and, seemingly out of the blue, her husband asked for a divorce and moved out of the family home. She was in a state of considerable shock and at a complete loss to understand why. She could not accept her husband's accusation that she had cut herself off from him and become impossible to relate to on an emotional level.

With such a fixed chart she found it difficult to adjust, and felt distraught, disorientated and out of control. As always, she took an intellectual and rational approach. Wishing, above all, to remain reasonable, friendly and on good terms with her husband, she hoped that astrology could help her work out how she could get him to change his mind. An alchemical approach suggests that, perhaps for some time, she had been 'stuck in the sky'. The Uranus transit, however unwelcome, was prompting her to complete the *sublimatio* process and come back to earth and to the level of human relationships.

Since Uranus was transiting her Ascendant, it is possible that Linda was unconsciously prompting her husband to act out the role of perpetrator. Her shock and distress were very real but it seems that she had, however unknowingly, found herself caught in a double bind between her resistance to change and the compulsion to escape from old patterns, from a marriage which had itself become 'stuck'. Very gradually, she began to realise that the old bonds with her husband had already been severed and that there was nothing she could do to get him back. Linda began to look forwards again and even to welcome the possibility of new beginnings and new opportunities.

Salma has natal Uranus on her Descendant in Sagittarius, ruler of her Midheaven in Aquarius. A Turkish woman living in a traditional Muslim family, her birth as a girl had been a disappointment to them. She longed to escape from the confines of her birth family and culture and to experience more freedom and autonomy. Uranus transited her MC when she was fifteen years old and Salma developed a strong attraction to a foreigner – a non-Muslim man. But when her family found out she was put under strict surveillance and confined to the family home. Her relationship with her mother, always difficult, deteriorated as her frustration grew. It seemed that there was nothing she could do to please her mother, and that she was always found wanting. It was not until she was twenty years old and transiting Uranus squared her natal Uranus that her family arranged what they believed to be a suitable marriage, and she was finally able to escape from her family home.

Salma first contacted me with a view to choosing an optimal date and time for the elected caesarean birth of her daughter. She was not interested in exploring her motivations for a procedure which was not medically necessary. Nor was she interested in discussing her relationship with her husband or her feelings as she prepared to become a mother for the first time. But she was very clear that she wished to use astrology to construct a perfect 'designer baby'. Her criteria were that her daughter should be loving, caring, attractive, not prone to weight gain and, most important of all, that she should be strongly attached to her and not travel abroad when she grew up. As we explored the astrological themes prevalent during the timeframe of the birth, Salma consistently questioned, disagreed with and rejected my suggestions, and finally broke off our sessions before the birth of her daughter. Reflecting on Salma's case, it seemed likely that history would repeat itself and, as she herself had failed to be perfect enough for her mother, she would find it difficult to love her daughter unreservedly, just as she was, and to build the emotional bonds which had so far eluded her.

As our relationship to Uranus transforms, old convictions, certainties and rigid stances soften. As we emerge from Uranus transits we become less dissociated, less autocratic, less clear but more human, with an increased understanding of, and compassion for, ourselves and others. Gradually, as the dew gathers and begins to descend back towards the earth, new insights and perspectives can be integrated on a personal level and gifted back to the world.

Endnotes
1. *The Emerald Tablet*: See Appendix I.
2. Waite, E.A. *Hermetic Museum*, Vol 2, pp.142.
3. Jung, C.G. *Memories, Dreams, Reflections*, pp.240-1.
4. Jung, C.G. (CW12) *Psychology and Alchemy*, p.69.
5. Edinger, E.F. *Anatomy of the Psyche*, p.142.
6. The Gospel according to Mark 8:36, King James Version.
7. Lowinsky, N.R. *The Devil and the Deep Blue Sea: Faust as Jung's Myth and Our*

Own, pp.167-9.

8. A complete understanding of the myth of Prometheus (whose name means 'foresight'), necessarily includes his brother Epimetheus ('hindsight'), whose wife Pandora was the first mortal woman, gifted to Epimetheus by the gods. She brought with her a wedding gift from Zeus, a gilded box which she was told never to open, but could not resist doing so. In that gilded box, Zeus, in retribution for the theft by Prometheus of the divine fire, had hidden everything that would forever inflict misery on humanity: hatred and evil, turmoil and strife, famine, sickness, disease, plagues and death. In Hesiod's Theogony, the daemons of the jar were personified as children of Eris. Only Hope remained trapped inside the box, to give comfort to mankind.

9. Lowinsky, N.R. *The Devil and the Deep Blue Sea: Faust as Jung's Myth and Our Own*, pp.167-9.

Chapter 7
Calcinatio: The Pluto Process

"Its strength is complete if it be turned into earth"[1]

Calcinatio is the fire process, which involves the intense heating of a substance to drive off water and all volatile constituents. After repeated cookings, everything flammable is burnt away and nothing is left but grey ash at the bottom of the flask.

The Lesser Calcinatio
The uncalcinated state is analogous to the naïve power principle, an unconscious archetypal force, a drive for dominance and an obsessive need for control. Superficially, this may serve us well enough but, sooner or later, transiting Pluto will aspect itself, a natal planet or angle. We meet our match and all hell breaks loose.

As Pluto becomes active an intensity starts to build deep in the unconscious until the tension of the suppressed energy becomes unbearable. The primitive power of the emotions which are eventually unleashed can take us completely by surprise. Inherited, ancestral and collective material emerges from the unconscious and threatens to consume us. As we become increasingly possessed, Pluto undermines our sense of ourselves as civilised and reasonable human beings. We are plunged into what can feel like an alien and terrifying underworld of intense survival anxiety and savage emotions such as rage, murderousness, jealousy, vengeance and obsessive power struggles.

In the *lesser calcinatio*, the individual becomes the conduit through whom the suppressed and rejected instincts of the collective unconscious are brought to the surface. If we identify with this unleashed, titanic power, and attempt to ride its waves, we may feel omnipotent, capable of anything. Equally, we may find ourselves targeted or scapegoated by others, and feel terrified and utterly powerless to do anything about it. Either way, as perpetrators or victims, we are in the grip of powerful unconscious complexes.

The ancient myth of Inanna, Queen of Heaven and Earth, and of her dark, underworld sister, Ereshkigal, comes closest to describing the meaning of Pluto in the birthchart.[2] Inanna represents passionate creative power. She embodies the fierce independence and never domesticated aspect of the feminine. As goddess of sexual love, Inanna celebrates her body, craving and taking, denying and destroying. In her Ereshkigal aspect she is terrifying to the ego of both genders. She represents the destructive-transformative side of the cosmic will, the abyss which is the ground of all being. She rules over everything which seems inexorably opposed to civilised life: fury, greed, spite, rage, raw instinctuality and destructive violence split off from consciousness, as well as the new life which emerges from her indiscriminating fires.

In the *calcinatio* process, we are burned by life. Pluto describes the drive, no matter what the cost, to bring to the surface and eliminate anything in the collective which has become poisonous, decayed or rotten. At root, Pluto describes the organic laws of the decay, death and regeneration of all living things. The fires of Pluto purge and regenerate. The many violent alchemical images of the *calcinatio* show burning, hell-fire, suffocation and immolation, the agony of dragons on fire writhing inside the flask, symbolising our confrontation with the life force itself. The dragon is a symbol of the unrecognised power of the instincts, which live through all of us in an untransformed or unconscious state.

The *calcinatio* is performed on the hungry, instinctual, primitive power of our emotions, which make an appearance *because* they are thwarted. We meet a force greater than ourselves and we cannot have what we want. Our superficial, ego constructed, will to power and control is defeated.

Pluto awakens the passions with an intensity beyond reason. People with earthy charts are often shocked by the power of the passions which erupt with the transits of Pluto. Airy souls who see themselves as civilised become anything but. For watery people the *calcinatio* is a drying out process. Waterlogged

Figure 41
The dragon of the instincts devours itself in the fire

or contaminated complexes are dried out and emotional confusions are transformed in the fire. We are no longer prepared to be ignored, dispossessed or disempowered.

Psychologically, this stage is very toxic. There can be intense experiences of betrayal and abandonment, grief beyond endurance, and feelings of total impotence. The rage of the suppressed and unintegrated feminine in our culture is unleashed in savage retribution, and we are consumed by it. It makes human relationships impossible and destroys everyone in our path.

The *calcinatio* has to be endured. The fire has to burn the fire until the conflict, defeat and suffering forces its own transformation. The only thing we can do is to try and keep the stopper in the bottle until, under intense pressure, whatever is mortal or corruptible is burned up. In this way, we play our own small part in purging the dark, corrupt forces and destructive emotions which invade the individual from the collective unconscious.

In Figure 42, the dragon devours itself in fire water, just as destructive emotions have to suffered until they burn themselves out.

Eventually, the intensity of the Pluto transit begins to wane and we become quieter. The fires of obsession quieten and we are left with nothing but dry ash and glass. We have been burned through and, with our fantasies of personal power and control stripped away, we come to a more realistic relationship with ourselves and with the world. It is said that all conflicts arise out of the tension between love and power, and that true love for another means a renunciation of power, whether this is painful or effortless, conscious

Figure 42
The dragon of the instincts destroys itself in the fire

or unconscious, intentional or unintentional. In the words of the contemporary poet and writer, Ben Okri, "The most authentic thing about us is our capacity to create, to overcome, to endure, to transform, to love and to be greater than our suffering".

The Greater Calcinatio

The symbolism of the *greater calcinatio* includes ash, glass, salt, bitterness and wisdom[3], all of which are relevant to the transformation of Pluto in the birth chart. Ash, glass and salt are symbols of purified matter in its eternal state, after being subjected to the refining fire. Purified matter is no longer flammable.

Ash The symbolism of ash is defeat and failure, the sackcloth and ashes of mourning. But in alchemy, ash also describes the immortal, indestructible residue, the supreme value which remains once the corrupt will to power has been burned up and destroyed. When our inordinate passions have been burned up we can walk through fire without being touched.

Glass is also a product of the intense heat of the calcinatio. The chief feature of glass is its transparency; we can see things through it. As a symbol of transformed consciousness, glass symbolises Pluto's function in a birth chart, once it has been truly calcinated. We emerge out of the *calcinatio* on another level altogether, with a certain immunity to affect. We can see through to the archetypal aspects of existence, to the truth of things, and absolute integrity replaces the will to personal power and control.

Salt is synonymous with the ash that is left at the end of the *calcinatio*. When the ashes are combined with water, they produce the alchemical Salt, a combination of the feminine elements of earth and water.

> "…. fire began to act on air, and produced *Sulphur*; air acted on water and produced *Mercury*; **water, by its action on earth, produced Salt.**"[4]

Salt was one aspect of the *tria prima*, or three alchemical principles: sulphur, mercury and salt, identified by Paracelsus with spirit, soul and body. The alchemists were clear that the *opus* could not succeed without salt. "No man can understand this Art who does not know the salt and its preparation".[5] The fixed part of the soul *desires nutrition and generation,*

Figure 43
The instincts, in the form of a lion, are purged and purified by fire, devoured by a toad and absorbed into the Moon, symbolising the feminine elements of earth and water.

and salt symbolises the inclusion of the redeemed feminine principle into the totality of the psyche.

The rich symbolism of salt pertains to the principle of the flesh, to individual, incarnated existence, to the feminine, as the 'white foliated earth' of many alchemical recipes.[6] Salt is the white earth, one of the basic human tastes, and essential for life. Salt symbolism extends to a commitment to life and to community, to realism and earthly engagement.

As D.H. Lawrence wrote in 1913:

"My belief is in the blood and flesh as being wiser than the intellect. The body-unconscious is where life bubbles up in us. It is how we know that we are alive, alive to the depths of our souls and in touch somewhere with the vivid reaches of the cosmos."

Bitterness and Wisdom
James Hillman writes that salt belongs to the history of our souls and is marked by its trauma; it is mined from the rocks of our life experiences, which are salted away and stored within. We tend to fixate on what has been done to us and who did it, in resentment, revenge, bitterness. But what matters psychologically is that it was done: the blow, the blood,

77

the betrayal. Salt is the experience of being alive and being in the world.

> "Salt symbolises the very essence of our lives, our felt experiences and deep hurts, the ground of our subjectivity. We make salt in our suffering and, by working through our sufferings we heal the soul of its salt deficiency. Our tears, sweat and blood are all salty, and our wounds are healed by the alchemical salt."[7]

The symbolism of salt is associated with the bitterness of real, incarnated existence. But wisdom is the other side of bitterness:

> "Apart from its lunar wetness and its terrestrial nature, the most outstanding properties of salt are bitterness and wisdom. The psychological factor common to both is the function of *feeling*. Tears, sorrow and disappointment are bitter, but wisdom is the comforter in all psychic suffering. Where there is bitterness wisdom is lacking, and where wisdom is there can be no bitterness. Salt, as the carrier of this fateful alternative, is coordinated with the nature of woman." [8]

Edward Edinger[9] writes that salt is synonymous with *Sapientia Dei*, personified as Sophia, the goddess of practical, embodied wisdom. Hidden from patriarchal Christianity, Sophia represents the vital integrity, intelligence and cosmic power of the life force in both its creative and destructive aspects, the rarely acknowledged wisdom of the feminine. For Thomas Aquinas[10] *Sapientia Dei* was the feminine counterpart of God.

Calcinatio – Pluto and the story of Demeter, Persephone and Hades
During the transits of the outer planets, the archetypal themes portrayed in the great myths can provide context, perspective and guidance.

The myth of Hades, Demeter and Persephone is one of the most important of the ancient Greek myths, and the transits of Pluto constellate many themes in this story. As with all myths, each character has its part to play, and the inclusion of Demeter and Persephone adds an extra dimension to our understanding of Pluto's function in the birth chart. Although Hades is the protagonist, it is Demeter and Persephone, and not Hades, who experience the pain, suffering and profound transformations described in this myth.

Pluto

Pluto's Greek name, Hades, means 'unseen', 'invisible', and for many years Pluto can remain a dumb note in the birth chart, hidden from consciousness, while life continues on the surface.

The word 'Plutos' means wealth and, as guardian of the Earth's buried treasure, Pluto represents the fertility and immense resources which lie in and under the earth.

But Pluto was also the lord of the realm of the living dead, the ghosts of the past. Planets in, and ruling, the eighth house describe our psychic inheritance, both ancestral and collective, and we ignore them at our peril.

In *Beware the Unhappy Dead*, D.H Lawrence gives poetic expression to the power of the living dead in the following verse:

"Oh, but beware, beware the angry dead.
Who knows, who knows how much our modern woe
is due to the angry, unappeased dead
that were thrust out of life, and now come back at us
malignant, malignant, for we will not succour them."

Demeter

Demeter is the goddess of agriculture, particularly the crops which nourish and sustain us and which are essential for life. She is an aspect of the ancient *great mother* who, in her triple form – Persephone (maiden), Demeter (mother) and Hekate (crone) – presides over the cycle of life, the creative, destructive and regenerating powers of nature.

The myth of Demeter tells how her ancient dominion over the realms of the sky, sea and underworld was overthrown and usurped by her Olympian brothers, Zeus, Poseidon and Hades, and how she and her sisters, Hera and Hestia, came to be domesticated.

It tells of Demeter's betrayal, when Hades became consumed by desire for her daughter Persephone and how, with her father Zeus's permission, Hades abducted her and took her to his underworld kingdom.

Distraught and inconsolable at the loss of her daughter, Demeter fell into a deep period of mourning. But, as in the case of so many women who, like Demeter, have been disempowered, passed over or ignored, her grief and feelings of powerlessness eventually gave way to an immense rage against Zeus for his betrayal. In an act of revenge and retribution, and in an effort to coerce Zeus to allow the return of her daughter, Demeter caused a terrible drought across the world, in which the people suffered and starved.[11]

The power of the enraged feminine is inexorable, and Zeus had no choice but to relent. An agreement was reached and Hades was forced to return Persephone to her mother for six months of every year, during which time Demeter allowed the crops to grow once again.

The mystical marriage is a central goal of the alchemical *magnum opus*, and throughout the alchemical writings and illustrations it is clear that the masculine and feminine principles are of equal value. Equilibrium can only be restored, and the cycles of life can only continue, when the power of the feminine is sufficiently recognised and honoured.

Persephone

As an aspect of Pluto in the birth chart, Persephone symbolises the irreversible metamorphosis from one phase of life to another, often unsought and unwelcome, often experienced as a violent abduction from the familiar and comfortable world that we know. During the transits of Pluto we can feel, like Persephone, as if the ground has opened up beneath our feet, and find ourselves plunging into the terrifying unknown depths of the previously unknown inner world of the soul. Persephone's ordeal describes her passage from girlhood to womanhood.

Figure 44
Kore and Pluto

Hades' symbol is the pomegranate, used throughout history and in virtually every religion to symbolise fertility, marriage and abundance. By ingesting some pomegranate seeds in the underworld, Persephone had become fertile. There was no going back, and from that time forth she had to divide her time between her mother and her husband.

But Persephone was transformed by her encounter with Hades from the 'Kore', daughter of Demeter, to the Queen of the Underworld. She symbolises the painful experiences which lead to the birth of maturity, acceptance and wisdom.

Persephone's marriage to Hades is a genuine *mysterium coniunctionis*. She becomes his equal, and through her the primal power of the great goddess is redeemed. As the goddess of wisdom, Sophia, or *sapientia dei*, Persephone became the guide and teacher of the souls of the dead and of the living.

Working with the *Calcinatio*

The *calcinatio* processes describe our encounter with the destructive and regenerative powers of the feminine principle. They describe the radical metamorphosis which occurs as our relationship to Pluto transforms.

Calcinatio themes are activated when when transiting Pluto aspects a planet or angle in the birth chart, the nodal axis, or its natal position, most noticeably at the waxing square (between the ages of thirty-six and forty-five, depending on the year of birth).[1]

Every birth chart is unique but, as a general rule, our first encounter with the primordial feminine occurs around the age of twenty-four, depending on the year of our birth,[2] when transiting Pluto makes a conjunction with natal Neptune. This is usually a time of low energy, which often coincides with relationship and/or health crises, as our souls are confronted with the reality of our incarnation. It is a time of deeper self-discovery as old assumptions, illusions and false fantasies are burned away.

In the intense fires of these experiences, a metamorphosis occurs. This transit can set our lives on a completely different path, and herald the beginning of a more realistic, mature and integrated engagement with the world.

People with a prominent Pluto, those with Scorpio on one of the angles, or with an emphasis of planets in Scorpio or in the eighth house, are familiar with this intensity and become used to constantly entering the fires and emerging, renewed, like the mythical phoenix. Every time one layer is burned off, more layers are revealed and, as they begin to come to the surface, they too must also be burned off. And so the process continues in the *circulatio*.

The transits of Pluto release the previously dormant, hidden power of the destructive and creative aspects of the feminine which, in our culture, have been systematically suppressed. The denied or sabotaged wisdom and intense passions of our mothers, grandmothers and female ancestors can be awakened and demand expression through us. The purging fires of the *calcinatio* can be empowering.

Initially, in the fires of the *calcinatio*, it is not unusual to become consumed by the fires of passion, jealously obsessed by another person. If the *calcinatio* is projected, we may find ourselves in the terrifying position of being the object of another person's obsession. Or we can feel, often for the first time, intense rage and the desire for vengeance and retribution, driven by an underlying grief that we have spent so much of our lives giving our power away to others.

Carole was a wife, mother, home-maker, breast-feeding councillor and member of the parent-child committee at her children's school; in short, a pillar of her community. Her natal Pluto/Moon conjunction lay dormant in the twelfth house, suggesting the dangerous aspects of Ishtar/Inanna, the hidden creative power, passion, destructive and creative aspects of the feminine which have been culturally suppressed and which had been denied and sabotaged by many generations of women in her family.

As transiting Pluto approached its square to her natal Pluto, it was time to release her unlived life, to live more dangerously and to explore her power as a woman. She became attracted to a man whom she met at her gym, an attraction which was initially reciprocated but, as he began to withdraw, gradually developed into an obsession. She had to have him. In the purging fires of the *calcinatio*, she embarked on a series of cosmetic surgeries and lost a great deal of weight in order to transform her appearance and become irresistible to him. As her obsession intensified, she began to stalk him, in order to find out more about his life and movements, and even posted gifts, cards and items of personal clothing through his letter box. For a while, her rage was directed towards his girlfriend, whose car she attacked one night in a fit of vengeance and jealousy. She was incapable of any kind of rational thinking and blind to the fact that he was unavailable. She was so consumed by the fires of her passion that she began working on a telephone sex line. Carole's behaviour became so extreme that she jeopardized everything in her life which had previously held value, her marriage and family life, something which would have been unthinkable a few years previously.

Eventually, her marriage did break up, and a new life began to emerge for her on the other side. Perhaps Pluto's role was to activate Carole's unconscious urge to escape the confines of her previously socially prescribed, dutiful and acceptable role as a wife and mother. Perhaps she was playing her own personal part in freeing the feminine in our culture, releasing the constraints of her inheritance in order to gain her autonomy and live more authentically, passionately and creatively.

The various stages of the *calcinatio* closely resemble the ancient rituals which re-enacted the mysteries of the seasonal death and regeneration of the vegetative cycles upon which life depends. The Eleusinian Mysteries belonged to the cult of Demeter and Persephone. They were secret rituals observed annually for two thousand years, from 1600 BCE until 392 CE, when they were closed down by the Christian Emperor Theodosius. They are believed to have involved a ritual re-enactment of the death and rebirth of Persephone.

Initiates would descend into an underground chamber, into the realm of the living dead, to die and be reborn. During a period of incubation, they would encounter the goddess within, and learn the truth of existence. It was said of those initiated at Eleusis that they emerged radically changed, in the realisation of eternal life and freed from the fear of death.

Jane was a forty-six-year-old woman with natal Pluto in the sixth house. She had met her husband when they were both medical students although, with the arrival of her children, she decided not to complete her training but to devote herself to the needs of her family. As her children grew up, she worked as a receptionist in her husband's medical practice. But transiting Pluto had now reached her MC, and her extremely demanding and powerful mother had recently died after a prolonged illness. Jane had anticipated that her mother's death would come as something of a relief but, as she began to adjust, she wanted to explore some new realisations and deeper feelings which had begun to emerge. Her unexpected grief seemed to go deeper and beyond her mother's death into something more universal and collective to do with the lives of women. She realised the extent to which her mother had dominated and controlled her life and how, by extension, she had subjected herself to her husband's control. She felt as if she had an unexploded bomb inside her. With Uranus simultaneously transiting her Ascendant in Pisces she was no longer content to work solely for her husband, but was gripped by a desire for more independence and autonomy. All the old docility and subservience were burning up and felt it was time, eventually, to step into her own power. Notwithstanding her husband's incomprehension, she began to develop a deep and abiding interest in helping women to navigate the cycles of life, birth and death, recognising that this was in fact a blocked legacy from her mother. She trained as a doula, and began to support women through their own transitions, through childbirth, miscarriages, stillbirths and dying. As she entered this new rich deep territory, she came into her power as a woman, and found great fulfilment working in service to the great mother.

Jasper was a sixty-three-year-old man with a Sun/Pluto conjunction in Leo on the IC. Born into a powerful and influential family, he had become wealthy and successful in his own right, used to taking it for granted that he would and could get what he wanted. With transiting Pluto now on his Descendant, he hoped that astrology could help him secure a potential relationship with a woman over twenty years younger than himself. After a few dates, during which he lavished her with expensive gifts, he was concerned that she seemed to be backing off but, just as in the case of Pluto and Persephone, he was determined to have her. He seemed to know almost nothing about her as a person, and did not appear to be interested in her feelings, thoughts, hopes or wishes. Rather, he wished to add her to his possessions. During the period when she was having her own Pluto square Pluto, he was having her followed by a private detective, and I can only imagine how terrified she must have been feeling.

Eventually, as the Pluto transit began to lose its intensity and he became quieter, Jasper started talking about his wife, who had died a few years previously, at the time of his second Saturn return and shortly after his retirement. It was clear that beneath his Pluto obsession lay a great deal of grief, both for the loss of his identity and status in the world, and for his wife, who had been everything to him. Throughout his life, the feminine principle had remained externalised in the figures of his mother, wife and now in his search for a partner.

Recognition of the destructive and creative power of Pluto is vital to transforming both ourselves and the world. By confronting our own depths, by meeting and burning through our own small inheritance of the dark and distorted unconscious forces of Pluto, we can transform its expression in our own lives and return it to the collective as a regenerated life force.

Provided that the alembic holds, we discover, when the Pluto transits pass, that, like the initiates in the Elusinian mysteries, we have come to know the goddess within our own souls, the ultimate source of our strength, support and wisdom.

Between them, the *Sublimatio* and *Calcinatio* operations bring about the confrontation, death, transformation and rebirth of these radically opposing principles, represented by Uranus and Pluto in the birth chart. They will be reunited in the *Solutio*, represented by Neptune in the birth chart, by the mediating forces of the soul, and eventually through their mystical marriage produce the divine child, the product of their union and the goal of the alchemical *opus*.

Endnotes

1. *The Emerald Tablet*, see Appendix I.
2. Perera, Silvia B. *Descent to the Goddess*, p.24.
3. Jung, C.G. (CW14) *Mysterium Coniunctionis*, paras.234-348.
4. Waite, E.A., *Hermetic Museum*, Vol 2, pp.142f.
5. Jung. C.G. (CW14) *Mysterium Coniunctionis* para.329.
6. ibid para.154, note 181.
7. Hillman, J. *A Blue Fire*, pp.117-120.
8. Jung, C.G. (CW14) *Mysterium Coniunctionis*, paras 315-348.
9. Edinger, E. *The Mysterium Lectures*, p.165.
10. Von Franz, M-L. (2000), *Aurora Consurgens*.
11. A remarkable contemporary parallel to the myth of the suppression and usurpation of the power of the primal feminine, is the demotion of Pluto's planetary status by the International Astronomical Union in 2008. Pluto has been reclassified, along with the asteroid Ceres (Demeter), as a dwarf planet. Pluto, Ceres, Eris, Haumea and Makemake are now just a few of the hundreds, perhaps thousands of dwarf planets belonging to the category of trans-Neptunian objects which lie in the outer regions of the solar system, within and beyond the region known as the Kuiper belt. The age-old myths of the disempowerment, dismemberment and banishment of the great mother have been re-enacted by the scientific community.

It is never wise to dismiss or underestimate the power of the feminine, and the inclusion of Eris as one of the dwarf planets is, perhaps, archetypally necessary. Eris was the goddess of chaos, strife and discord, goddess of the battlefield with an insatiable desire for revenge. Just as Pluto has been excluded from the planetary pantheon, Eris was excluded from attending the wedding of Peleus and Thetis, and her rage and retribution followed. The Hawaiian fire goddess Haumea was the goddess of fertility and childbirth, divine creatrix and spirit of mother nature. As in the myth of Demeter, her story includes the cultivation of the land, and the reliance of mankind on the food which mother nature produces. The earth is her body, including the volcanoes which run along the islands of Hawaii and continue to erupt, the lava burning everything in its path. She was said to influence those whose lives were filled with burning anger against their fellow men. Makemake is a male fertility god and creator of humanity, associated with the mythology of Easter Island.

12. See Appendix II.
13. ibid.

Chapter 8
Solutio: The Neptune Process

"From here will come the marvellous adaptations, whose manner this is."[1]

In the alchemical *solutio* the material in the flask is heated until it melts or dissolves into a liquid, as if it had been swallowed up. The phrase *solve et coagula* describes the constantly repeated operations of dissolving what is fixed and coagulating what is volatile, separating and re-uniting, since '*only separated things can unite*'.

Neptune in the birth chart describes the undifferentiated part of us which remains in the *prima materia*, unknown and unborn, still immersed in the collective unconscious.

Through Neptune we are subjected to, and unconsciously continue to perpetrate, the accumulated emotions and longings which reside in the ancestral and collective memory. These can include an exquisite sensitivity to beauty, joy and love, but Neptune also carries the residues of unfinished business, unresolved suffering, pain and overwhelming grief.

Lesser Solutio
Neptune describes the all too human longing to regress, to be dissolved, to merge with something – anybody or anything – which we believe will heal our existential wounds of separateness and isolation. Neptune transits trigger intense emotions as we surrender into a state of fusion, seduced by fantasies of divine union or redemption.

We yearn to return to an idealised imaginary past, to the womb, to a state of passive symbiosis where all our needs for containment, support, nourishment and unconditional love are spontaneously fulfilled. We become particularly susceptible to falling in love, or under the spell of any organisations, social or spiritual ideologies, in the embrace of which we believe our suffering and isolation will be dissolved. But in our delusional state we may not realise that we are being taken down into the waters and drowned. Neumann observes that, for an immature, 'unsolved' ego, the blissful *solutio* is very destructive:

Figure 45
The devouring nature of the *solutio*

"In uroboric incest, the emphasis upon pleasure and love is in no
sense active, it is more a desire to be dissolved and absorbed; passively
one lets oneself be taken, sinking into the pleroma, melting away in
the ocean of pleasure. The Great Mother takes the little child back
into herself, and always over uroboric incest there stands the insignia
of death, signifying final dissolution in union with the Mother."[2]

The dissolving, devouring aspect of the great mother calls to us through
our fantasies, delusions and addictions, most commonly to relationships,
work, drugs and alcohol, even to the point of suicide. This is a form of
artificial *solutio* and it is, of course, immensely powerful and seductive.
Like psychic vampires, our addictions devour and feed off us, just as
we devour and feed off them. The *lesser solutio* can be identified by its
parasitic behaviour. It is driven by lust, by the craving of the ego to
consume the object of its desire. But the bliss of regression into the
original *prima materia* is not the object of the alchemical *opus*.

Neptune also describes where and how we stubbornly refuse to face
reality or to engage with the world as separate from us. Neptune has hazy

energetic boundaries which obscure the question of who is doing what to whom. Consciously or unconsciously, we refuse to be seen, using all manner of camouflage or smoke screens to generate false illusions and chaos. Harnessing Neptune to our own ego purposes, we demand that the world and other people conform to our will. There are many subtle but powerful ways of attempting to control others in order to get what we want.

Until the ego has been dissolved in the alchemical bath, we fail to realise that our dreams and delusions are overwhelmingly narcissistic. In refusing to accept our separateness, we use coercion, manipulation, deception and seduction to get our own way. Feeding off the unresolved past, we continue to poison ourselves and others as we are repeatedly drawn to situations guaranteed to result in more pain. Addicted to our suffering, we develop as art forms a range of subtle and not so subtle demonstrations of self-sacrifice or martyrdom, designed to justify our actions.

Eventually, in the *lesser solutio*, the ego is dissolved in the alchemical bath. The dissolving of our illusions and fantasies is often accompanied by overwhelming feelings of abandonment and a period of grieving and mourning for the loss of the ivory tower which has previously supported us. We feel cast out, alone and rejected by the gods who used to spin the web for us.

As always, the symbolism of the alembic is crucial, since it is the containing vessel within which the transformation will take place. The alembic is portrayed throughout the alchemical images of *solutio* as a dissolving bath, a sarcophagus or tomb, a womb and, finally, a font. In the tomb the opposites die to their separateness, in the womb the new life gestates, and in the font it is baptised, or sanctified. Neptune fulfils all these functions at different times in our lives, in the *circulatio*.

Many repeated experiences of the *solutio* are needed before Neptune has been sufficiently cleansed and released from the accumulated weight of human history.

In our culture we do not recognise or value the natural ebb and flow of the soul's engagement with our lives, with all its joys and sufferings. During the solutio we are forced to turn inwards, no matter how painful that may be, and in that process to meet our deeper selves.

Experienced as periods of meaninglessness, melancholy or depression, we are generally unable to accept that periods of contraction, contemplation and retreat may be absolutely necessary, providing opportunities to rest and re-couperate (literally to 're-gather') and to re-member (literally to 're-connect' with) ourselves.

An alchemical approach to astrological work provides a context for such dark nights of the soul. The alchemists knew that periods of meaninglessness, despair, heaviness or exhaustion were an inevitable and necessary part of the *opus*, and would reoccur many times in the process of the *circulatio*. Seen in this light, they can be understood as being essentially initiatory, as we meet at last the essential characteristics of our own souls.

The ability to identify and validate these periods within an astrological context can be the most helpful and ultimately therapeutic approach we can take. The influence of the outer planets teaches us that there are other realms and dimensions to human life, the realisation of which releases us from the social treadmill, on which we are expected to be fully engaged with the world, a useful cog in the social, industrial or corporate machines, or whatever it is that our family or culture wants from us.

Periods of exhaustion, chronic fatigue, grief and mourning can be valid *solutio* experiences, particularly when they have no obvious physical or emotional cause. The *solutio* process is absolutely necessary if we are

Figure 46
The soul separating from the body

to overcome our estrangement from ourselves, from others and from the world. The deepest *solutio* experiences can be caused by relationships which break our hearts. But gradually, as we come to value the heart, we become capable of a less self-absorbed, less narcissistic kind of loving.

The Greater Solutio

In the *greater solutio* the previously unconscious, often self-destructive, influences of Neptune are softened or dissolved. Neptune transits can be understood as opportunities for the ruling principle of consciousness to drown in the deep waters of the soul, where the unconscious, inherited distortions can be cleansed, where we can re-collect ourselves and, when the time is right, re-enter the world with a more integrated understanding of our own natures.

One alchemical recipe for *solutio* is the following:

"Dissolve sol and luna in our dissolving water, which is familiar and friendly, and as it were a womb, a mother, the beginning and end of their life. And because sol and luna have their origin from this water their mother, it is necessary therefore that they enter into it again, into their mother's womb, that they may regenerate or be born again, and made more healthy, more noble and more strong."[3]

In the *greater solutio* we come to realise that all our attempts to remain merged, unborn, have in fact kept us strangers from our capacity to relate, to feel and to genuinely love ourselves and others for who we or they actually are. Unconditional love and compassion can only be achieved after a long process of discrimination and analysis, during which we learn to accept the reality of the opposites within.

"For one human being to love another: that is perhaps the most difficult of all our tasks … Love is not anything that means merging, giving over, and uniting with another (for what would a union be of something unclarified and unfinished, still subordinate?) – it is a high inducement to the individual to ripen, to become something in himself, to become world, to become world for himself for another's sake, it is great exacting claim upon him, something that chooses him out and calls him to vast things."[4]

The Mercurial part of the Soul

The mutable, *mercurial* part of the soul is a combination of the positive, masculine element of air and the negative, feminine element of water.

> ".... fire began to act on air, and produced *Sulphur*; **air acted on water and produced Mercury**; water, by its action on earth, produced *Salt*."[5]

Mutable souls, those with an emphasis of planets in Gemini, Virgo, Sagittarius and Pisces, are fertile, fluid and flexible. They involve themselves in a flow of impressions, reflections and connections, which are themselves in a state of constant flux. They thrive in the ebb and flow of life, dancing between the opposites, constantly adapting and adjusting as they interact with their environment. The mutable part of the soul separates and reunites the opposites, spirit and matter, sulphur and salt, Uranus and Pluto.

When the principle of Neptune is made conscious in an individual, we can outgrow our personal feelings of separateness and isolation and come to realise that we are, and always have been, contained in, and supported by, the *anima mundi*, the soul of the world. The *greater solutio*, as the universal solvent, carries the promise of a joyful, loving connection to the transpersonal dimension of our nature, to our souls. Through the *greater solutio* we find the courage to turn again towards life, with an open heart, whatever the cost.

Figure 47 is from the famous Ripley Scroll, and graphically illustrates the central position of the soul, in the figure of the *mercurial* dragon, both separating and uniting the spirit above and the world below. The spiritual, masculine part of the soul rests in the cradle of the Moon. The material, feminine part of the soul is revivified by the wings of spirit and receives its life blood from the heart of the soul.

In the *greater solutio*, the opposites are consciously reconciled and reunited, no longer in lust but in love, a process which leads to rejuvenation and immersion in the creative flow of life.

The marriage of these two dimensions of reality eventually leads to the birth of the divine child, the *filius macrocosmi*, "the awakened consciousness that is the ultimate fruit of this union."[6]

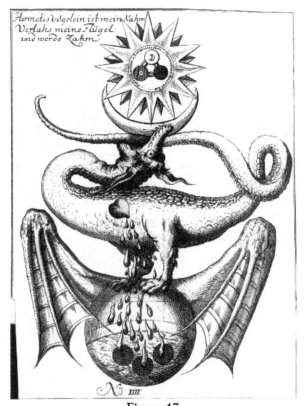

Figure 47
The spiritual and material parts of the soul, separated and united in love by
the mercurial dragon.

Neptune and the myth of Psyche and Eros

The alchemical transformation of Neptune in the birth chart can be
told through the myth of Psyche and Eros, the Greek personifications of
soul and love.

This is a fundamentally alchemical myth, since it describes the
radical transformation of both parties, male and female, personified by
Eros and Psyche. It is an archetypal journey, describing how our initial
unconscious polarisation and alienation from ourselves is gradually
outgrown, how we emerge from the swamps of inherited fantasies and
delusions and how, in the process, we come to know and love our own
souls.

The Greek word *psyche* means 'soul, spirit, breath, life or animating
force'. It also means 'butterfly', a creature which goes through a pro-

found metamorphosis. Psyche was a human princess of exquisite grace and beauty, worshipped and adored from afar as an ideal, a muse, an unattainable image of mortal beauty.

Aphrodite was the goddess of embodied sexuality, fertility and procreation, associated with pleasure, passion and desire, a Greek development of the more ancient Sumerian cult of Inanna/Ishtar. But she also represented the concept of courtship, where partners gradually grow to know and love one another. Psyche's ethereal, virginal and untouchable beauty was offensive to Aphrodite. A disembodied fantasy of the idealised and perfect woman, Psyche was no more than a muse, an *anima* figure, a projection of men's souls onto an outside form.

Aphrodite is almost always accompanied by her son Eros, immature god of love, still bound to his mother. It was Eros, whose magical arrows incited lust, mindless desire, and unrelated sex. The Greek lyric poets regarded his power as dangerous, compulsive and impossible to resist.

Aphrodite sent Eros to shoot Psyche with one of his arrows to make her fall hopelessly in love with the first man she saw, no matter how wretched, unsuitable or unappealing he might be. Intent on carrying out his mother's wishes, Eros accidentally pricked himself with his own arrow, and fell in love with Psyche himself.

Afraid of angering his mother, Eros spirited Psyche away to a fantasy paradise, and visited her in secret every night and only after dark. He promised Psyche anything she wished for, on condition that she agreed never to look at him, and never to ask any questions, conditions to which Psyche agreed. Not knowing herself, she must not ask to know him.

At this point in the myth, both Psyche and Eros are unformed, unconscious and therefore incapable of truly loving each other. Their relationship was a mutual fantasy. They were blind, caught in the enchantment and delusion of being in love, in the *lesser solutio*. Eros was pure puer aeternus; he wanted his paradise but without encumbrances or responsibility. He wanted Psyche to be there for him to come home to, but insisted on the freedom to come and go as he chose. In her collusion, Psyche subjected herself to his hidden domination. Many women allow themselves to be seduced in order to get what they want, just as many men satisfy their desires through unrelated sex.

But in all good myths there is a fly in the ointment, a worm in the apple, and Psyche's two sisters represented the doubts and nagging voices, within and without, which became the initial agents of her awakening. They had heard that Psyche's husband was a god, but, when they visited her she was unable to answer any of their questions, and told them that she had never seen his face. Suggesting that Psyche's unknown lover could be a monster, they provided her with an oil lamp and a knife, encouraged her to look on his face while he was sleeping and, if he was indeed a monster, to take the knife and cut off his head.

For a relationship to become conscious and real, both the lamp and the knife are necessary. The lamp symbolises our willingness to take a good look at someone we are close to. But the lamp is no good without the knife, a symbol of discrimination, the ability to cut through the fantasy and, if what we see in the light of the lamp is negative, to end a relationship by severing its bonds.

When Psyche raised the lamp and looked at her unknown bridegroom for the first time, she saw, to her utter amazement and bewilderment, that he was the god of love and the most beautiful creature on all of Mount Olympus. Robert Johnson writes that, "for a woman to evolve, she must break the unconscious domination of her own inner masculine, which dictates her relationship to the outer world. When, with the lamp of her consciousness, a woman actually sees her lover for what he is, she learns how to relate to him and is no longer subservient."[7]

Figure 48
Psyche and Eros

But a drop of oil fell from the lamp onto Eros' shoulder and he awoke to find her poised over him, knife in hand. Hurt and angry, and blaming Psyche for her betrayal and lack of trust, he flew back home to his mother, to whom he made a full confession. Johnson writes that, if a man feels unready or incapable of living up to a woman's newly realised consciousness, he will leave.

Abandoned, alone and feeling unable to cope, Psyche wandered the earth, looking for her lost love and eventually she approached Aphrodite, begging for the return of her husband and for her blessing on the marriage. Aphrodite demanded that Psyche complete four tasks, each more frightening and difficult than the one before, but each of which were important stages in her inner development, if she were to prove worthy of marriage to her son.

Psyche's first reaction to every task was despair, but each task contained important lessons designed to help her grow beyond what she knew before. The Psyche myth is a metaphor for psychological growth, the lessons that we need to learn if we are to become truly capable of loving another as an ordinary human being, stripped of fantasy projections. It describes an archetypal journey of initiation to maturity, during which we must learn to face our fears, trust our instincts, develop personal agency and function intelligently and strategically in the world.

First Task

Psyche's first task was to sort all the seeds that were heaped up in a room. This is a seemingly small task, but one which demands practical capabilities, including patience and discrimination, and the ability to create and restore order. Sorting and separating involves making conscious choices. Alchemically, this relates to the necessary process of *separatio*. It is not an intellectual task, but a practical one, and in the myth Psyche was helped by an army of ants, representing our natural instincts.

Second Task

Psyche's second task was to gather some of the golden fleece from the rams of the sun, and bring it to Aphrodite. The rams were powerful, strong and aggressive, and Psyche realized that she would be trampled in the attempt. Stealing the golden fleece represents masculine heroism, the ability to overcome and overpower through overt confrontation and competition. But there are other ways to gain power, through the intelligent use of strategy and the ability to observe and bide one's time, acting when the time is right, rather than confronting head on that which would otherwise destroy us.

Down on the riverside, a reed told Psyche that, if she waited until nightfall, when the rams were quieter, she could pick some of the fleece which had been caught on the bushes and trees, and fulfil her task. The reed symbolises a particular kind of strength, since it survives and thrives by bending with the flow of water.

Third Task
For her third task, Aphrodite gave Psyche a crystal jar and demanded that she fill it with water taken from the River Styx. When she saw the tremendous danger involved, Psyche once again fell into the depths of despair, but an eagle, circling above her, swept down for the jar, flew to the river and filled it for her.

The eagle is Zeus' bird, and represents the ability to gain perspective, to see the picture from above. This task relates to the importance of gaining emotional distance, to pick out the essential details and to grasp what is truly significant.

Fourth Task
For her fourth task, Aphrodite commanded that Psyche enter the underworld, fill an empty box with beauty ointment from Persephone, Queen of the Underworld, and return it to her.

Overcome by the impossibility of such a task, Psyche prepared to throw herself off a high tower to die, the only way she knew how to get into the underworld. But the tower provided her with the necessary information to help her prepare properly for the journey so that she could see it through and return. If she was to complete her task, she would need the strategy and resources not only to enter the underworld, but to repeat the whole process in reverse on her way back.

The tower is a human construction, representing social conventions, rules, traditions and systems. The tower gave her strategic advice. It told her to take two coins for the ferryman, one to let her into the underworld and one to let her out again, and two cakes for the three-headed dog

Cerberus, one to let her into the underworld and one to let her out again. It warned her that she would be asked for help three times, but must harden her heart to pity, refuse, and go on. The final piece of advice from the tower was not to open the box containing the beauty ointment. One of the hardest lessons for many women is to learn to prioritise their own needs rather than to allow themselves to be constantly imposed upon and diverted from tasks that are meaningful to them. Many women become exhausted from taking on too many responsibilities, but Psyche's journey into the underworld and back demanded courage, determination and resourcefulness and, if she was to succeed, she had to conserve her energy, curb her generosity and learn to say no.

She must refuse to assist a lame donkey driver who would ask her to pick up some sticks. She must refuse the groping hand of a drowning man as he reached up out of the water, and she must refuse to assist the three women who were weaving the threads of fate. In other words, she must resist the temptation to rescue others at her own expense, or to get involved in the weaving of other people's lives. She will serve them better by attending to her own fate. Psyche remembered the warning and ignored the three pleas for help.

Psyche managed to complete all her tasks and to return to the upper world but, just as she was within reach of achieving her goal, she opened the box and a death-like sleep enveloped her. Overwhelmed once again by the unconscious, she fell down as if dead.

It was this event which called Eros to her side, but this is a very different Eros from the god who abandoned her. As Psyche had grown through her ordeals, so Eros had transformed from a youth, still dependent on his mother, into a mature and independent male, capable of real commitment and willing to support and protect his loved one. This final act reveals that the mystical marriage must be a conscious union of true equals.

Figure 49
Psyche revived by Cupid's kiss

Realising that he truly loved Psyche – his soul – Eros wiped the death-like sleep off her, returned it to the casket and closed the lid. He no longer wished for her to remain unconscious.

This time he approached Zeus for help, the king of the gods, rather than his mother. Zeus was aware that the couple loved each other and transformed Psyche into a goddess in her own right. Psyche had earned her immortality and, in the presence of all the gods and goddesses on Mount Olympus, Zeus legitimized their marriage. Eros declared his love for Psyche and Aphrodite gave her blessing to the union.

The Olympians celebrated the grand wedding between Soul and Love, and from their union, their *mysterium coniunctionis*, a child was born. Their daughter was named Voluptas, or Hedone (the Greek root of the word 'hedonism'), meaning sensual pleasure, bliss and delight.

Working with the *Solutio*
Neptune spends around fourteen years in each sign, and carries the dreams and longings of each successive generation. For the Neptune in Libra and Scorpio generations, for example, the *solutio* processes are normally experienced through relationships. For the generation with Neptune in Sagittarius, the ideal is always calling from beyond, from somewhere else, engendering a restless search for new horizons, new meaning, new gods to serve. With Neptune in Capricorn, there is an unfulfilled desire for more stability, status and security. Neptune's house describes the area of life in which we invest our dreams, the ivory tower where we are unconsciously separated from, but dreaming about, life.

Natal Neptune on the angles suggests an inability or unconscious refusal to engage with the practical restrictions and ordinary realities of the world at large. With Neptune on the Ascendant or in the first house the energetic interface between ourselves and the world may be particularly hazy. Constructing an imaginative or glamourous self-image, a smoke screen behind which we hide, we may be unconsciously subjected to, or perpetrators of, seduction, manipulation and deception. Neptune on the IC or in the fourth house suggests great sensitivity to our early environment, and personal disorientation as we absorb the family atmosphere and unconsciously perpetuate the family patterns.

With Neptune on the Descendant or in the seventh house, our longing to merge with the other is driven by romantic fantasies. This protects us from having to develop the self definition and self knowledge needed in order to make a realistic commitment to another person. Unconsciously throwing up a veil of illusion between ourselves and others, we can all too easily deceive others or be deceived by them. With Neptune on the Midheaven or in the tenth house, we can be overwhelmed and subsumed by what we imagine the world demands of us, and end up feeling used, manipulated and burnt out.

Solutio processes are activated by the transits of Neptune to the planets, nodal axis and angles in the natal chart, most noticeably when Neptune squares its natal position, around the age of forty-two.

During Neptune transits, the fixities in our lives, our previous assumptions about ourselves and the world, are dissolved and broken down. Equally, the previously merged and formless aspects of our lives begin to take shape. Neptune dissolves that which is solid, and makes solid that which is dissolved. It is time for one form to disappear and a new, regenerated form to emerge.

Dreams and images of water, tidal waves, the sea, floods, rivers and drowning, can indicate that the solutio process has begun. Neptune transits are Dionysian, bringing life without measure and periods of exquisite ecstasy and bliss. But for some people they can be intensely painful, as familiar forms or structures melt away, and they lose their customary clarity, detachment and perspective. As the ability to find intellectual or rational solutions to problems recedes, they can be overwhelmed by periods of exhaustion or depression, or the prolonged shedding of tears, often with no obvious or recognisable cause. As the flood of the solutio grows, the loss of agency, direction and focus can cause intense anxiety and, if the level of fear and resistance is particularly pronounced, it can lead to a breakdown of some sort, or to obsessive, ritualised activities in an attempt to keep the impending chaos at bay.

But Neptune transits can also help us gain definition. With the aid of Psyche's lamp, we can begin to see, often for the first time, how we have been caught in a dream world, a fantasy paradise or swamp which has been so much more powerful than the reality. We may begin to realise that we have used our addictions to shield ourselves from the reality.

We begin to see how we have allowed our personal boundaries to be energetically invaded, and how the blind perpetuation of unfulfilled dreams and longings has been unconsciously inherited from our parents and ancestors. Not realising that it is our own souls which need rescuing, we devote our lives to trying to rescue others at our own expense, which can only lead to exhaustion and chronic fatigue.

Or we may realise for the first time how, pierced by Eros' arrow, we have fallen hopelessly in love with someone we do not see clearly and do not know. Instead, we have fallen in love with the god, with the fantasy of love itself. Caught in the enchantment, we may have unknowingly allowed ourselves to be deceived, manipulated, betrayed and abused.

Carole has a Sun/Neptune/Venus stellium in Sagittarius conjunct her Midheaven. She first consulted me when she was thirty-eight, at her Neptune square Neptune. Her family were Irish Catholics and her charismatic and charming father was an alcoholic. Her parents' marriage broke up when she was four years old, and Carole became a helper at a young age, trying to support her mother through all her emotional ups and downs through a series of affairs. Carole had always had a great interest in other cultures and religions, and a degree in Arabic Studies, but found herself working in the film industry, in an environment which, in many ways, reflected the chaos and financial uncertainties of her childhood. Her work was extremely demanding and for a while she tried to be all things to all people, but found herself getting increasingly exhausted, burned out. She felt that her life was out of control. Deeply in debt, and unable to pay off her loans, she began to drink heavily.

She had recently fallen passionately in love with a film director and turned to astrology to explore whether this longed-for relationship could become a reality. As transiting Neptune squared her stellium in Sagittarius, the pain of early abandonment by her adored and much-loved father came to the fore. Inherited family patterns are extremely powerful, and history has a way of repeating itself. Once again, Carole was feeling the pain of longing for a relationship with a charming and charismatic man who, like her father, would never be there for her.

Eventually, as the transit passed, her fantasies about the film director gradually dissolved and, with a broken heart, she began to emerge on the other side with a more defined and realistic sense of herself. Carole left the film industry and, returning to her interest in other cultures and religions, found work in an international humanitarian agency. Here, she found new purpose and focus in a profession where her contribution was valued and respected. She was able to stop drinking and gradually paid off her debts.

With Psyche's discriminating knife, we can cut through the fantasies and delusions and, as our projections dissolve, see other people more clearly, for who and what they are. As Psyche's task was to learn to say no, we realise that it is no longer necessary or appropriate to sacrifice our own goals to the needs of others. We begin to see our own habitual patterns of self-sacrifice and self-sabotage, and recognise at last the extent of our betrayal of ourselves and others. Breaking old relationship patterns is painful and can bring grief and heartbreak, and it is not unusual for people to feel guilt, shame or anger with themselves for their unconscious collusion. But this can be a necessary part of the process of extracting ourselves from our addictions and from toxic relationships.

Sarah's natal Neptune is conjunct the IC in Sagittarius. When Neptune transited her Descendant in Pisces and squared its natal position, hitherto blocked memories of her childhood began to surface. The family myth was one of a close, loving and caring unit, but Sarah began to see more clearly the hidden patterns of psychological and emotional abuse which existed behind this smokescreen. She realised that her personal boundaries had always been energetically invaded, particularly by her father, who had consistently manipulated and controlled her. Sarah had taken the role of family scapegoat, and periods of depression in her childhood had led her to become addicted to anti-depressants.

Sarah began to see her own patterns of self-sabotage, how she had allowed herself to be manipulated and how, for so many years, she had played the role of victim. She was angry with herself and felt guilty and ashamed of her collusion with the family system. She wished, more than anything, to break the old cycle of defining herself primarily through relationships. Only then, she felt, could she find true love.

Sarah's marriage repeated the old themes of collusion, manipulation and emotional abuse and, as her old identity dissolved, so did her twenty-year long marriage. Sarah felt real grief and heartbreak as she mourned the breakdown of her marriage but, as she pushed her husband away, she recognised that she could not change him, and that she could only change herself. Lost in the *solutio*, Sarah felt displaced from the outside world and from other people, but she was also aware that, very gradually, her familiar depression was lifting. Sarah felt a strong desire for solitude, to go on a pilgrimage, to get to know herself at last and to make a connection with her own soul. She longed to find a refuge and a retreat away from it all, where she could live closer to nature and find peace.

Melanie has a Sun/Neptune/Mercury conjunction in Scorpio in the sixth house. From a young age she had been fascinated by mythology and was always at her happiest when she could lose herself in stories of magical worlds. She studied psychology at university, where she met and had a long-term secret affair with one of her professors, who was married, but who professed that he could not live without her. Under his influence, she decided to train as a clinical psychologist, although this approach did not sit well with her deeper instincts or with her personal interests in myth, symbolism and the power of the imagination. Melanie found her work draining and, when transiting Neptune squared her natal Neptune, her affair ended and she had what she referred to as a complete breakdown of body, mind and spirit. For several years she was overwhelmed with chronic fatigue and unable to work.

As Melanie began to recover, problems in the family business began to emerge. Systematic thefts over a long period of time had brought the business to the brink of bankruptcy, and the stress was seriously affecting her father's health. She was considering whether she should now throw herself into the family business to support her father and to try and sort out the financial problems. With her Sun, Neptune, Mercury conjunction in Scorpio in the sixth house, it is easy to understand why she felt this way, but she was well aware that she could not afford to risk jeopardizing her health again. Mindful that one of Psyche's tasks was to refuse the groping hand of a drowning man, she determined to extend her loyalty and friendship to her father, but to maintain her distance from the business. Only by doing so could she attend at last to her own fate and begin to live her own life.

In the light of Psyche's lamp, we gain perspective and emotional distance. No longer compelled to live through others, we discover our inner resources, learn to priorities our own needs and, in the process, to be true to our own souls. We become truly capable of loving another as an ordinary human being, just as they are, stripped of fantasy projections.

As Dane Rudhyar writes: "The ghosts and shadows of the past will vanish when subjected to the light of understanding and compassion."[8]

Emerging with a more defined and realistic sense of ourselves, and with a newfound loyalty to our own souls, so too the magical and mysterious realms of the imagination and of the other worlds are released from personal and ancestral contamination. Our psychic connections grow stronger and are freed up for joyous exploration.

Endnotes
1. *The Emerald Tablet*, Appendix 1.
2. Neumann, E. *The Origins and History of Consciousness*, p.17.
3. Artefius, in Waite, A.E. *Lives of the Alchemystical Philosophers*, pp.145-46.
4. Rilke, R.M. *Letters to a Young Poet*, Penguin Classics (2016).
5. Waite, E.A. *Hermetic Museum*, Vol 2, pp.142f.
6. Baring, A. *The Dream of the Cosmos*, p.465.
7. Johnson, R. *She: Understanding Feminine Psychology*, p.42.
8. Rudhyar, D. *The Astrological Houses*, p.133.

Figure 50
The Mystical Marriage

Sol and Luna, the king and the queen, are reunited in the vessel containing the waters of life. The twinned serpent, or *caduceus*, symbolises the differentiation and union of opposites. The crowned mercurius figure, as *filius hermaphroditus*, stands above, holding the caduceus and staff, or wand. The six planets surround the font.

Chapter 9
Coniunctio: The Mystical Marriage and the Philosophers' Stone

"Here is the strong power of the whole strength; for it overcomes every subtle thing and penetrates every solid. Thus the world has been created. From here will come the marvellous adaptations, whose manner this is."[1]

In alchemy, the three stages of the *coniunctio* correspond to the ascent of the tetractys from four to three, from three to two and from two to one, culminating in the creation of the Philosophers' Stone.

"Whoever would be a student of this sacred science must know the marks whereby these three Principles [Sulphur, Mercury and Salt] are to be recognised and also the process by which they are developed. For as the three Principles are produced out of four, so they, in their turn, must produce two, a male and a female; and these two must produce an incorruptible one, in which are exhibited the four [elements] in a highly purified and digested condition, and with their mutual strife hushed in unending peace and good will".[2]

Jung believed that the archetype of wholeness was in the process of being constellated in the collective psyche, but that it could only operate positively if it was made conscious in the individual human being. Jung named this archetype the *Anthropos*, an image of the Self, of the human being in which male and female, spirit, soul and matter, are genuinely united and through whom not only humankind but also reconciled.

"The Age of Aquarius will generate individual water carriers. The individual psyche is and must be a whole world within itself in order to stand over and against the outer world and fulfil its task of being a carrier of consciousness. The psyche will no longer be carried by religious communities but by conscious individuals."[3]

The first stage of the *coniunctio*

The first stage of the return journey was known as the *unio mentalis*, the reunion of spirit and soul, Uranus and Neptune, accompanied by a separation from the body and from nature. This is a spiritualizing process, closely resembling the symbolism of *sublimatio*, as if the soul and spirit want nothing to do with the body.

The *unio mentalis* is an abstract, idealised state of purity and perfection, known to the alchemists as the *albedo*, or whiteness, and to psychology as a state of inflation. It is not life in the true sense of the word, since everything individual, personal and self-centred has been left behind in the material residue.

A focus on the eternal realm of the spirit and transcendence from the natural world and from the body are a common theme in many religious traditions. In Christianity, the Christ figure descends from above to below, and returns to the above. But in alchemy it is clear from the Emerald Tablet that the journey is reversed. The *filius macrocosmi* starts

Figure 51
The reunion of the soul and the body

from below, ascends on high and, with the powers of the above and below united in himself, returns to earth again.[4]

The second stage of the *coniunctio*

The purpose of the second stage of the *coniunctio* is to bring the now united spirit and soul into a living, functioning, embodied personal reality. The life force itself still remains in the residue, and must be rescued. Spiritual, intellectual and theoretical abstractions are tempered as the soul is brought into a conscious relationship with the body and with all of nature.

The story of the union, mutual surrender and integration of the archetypal opposites, Uranus and Pluto, spirit and body, is illustrated in a series of twenty woodcuts from the *Rosarium Philosophorum*. The alchemical king and queen both die in the womb of the soul, where they become merged, one into the other. This is a graphic representation of the alchemical mixing of two different chemical substances. If there is any combination at all, both are transformed.

In the *Rosarium Philosophorum*, the process takes place in two sequences, each involving seven stages with the same archetypal form. In the first sequence, the crowned king and queen, with the aid of mercurius in the form of a bird, descend into the watery vessel, the unconscious realm of the inner life of the soul.

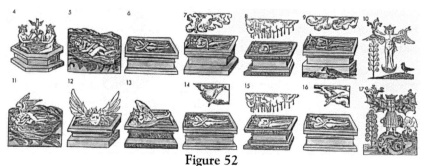

Figure 52

Images of the alchemical integration of opposites from the *Rosarium Philosophorum*

In the vessel, alchemical bath, or alembic, the previously polarised masculine and feminine aspects of the soul act upon each other and dissolve.

They are shown, lying in a sarcophagus, now fused into a hermaphrodite with one body and two heads. The hermaphrodite symbolises the marriage of opposites, the synthesis where two become one. In each sequence there are four images of the hermaphrodite lying in the sarcophagus, seemingly dead, drowned in the waters of the *solutio*. The container, initially a tomb, will eventually transform into a womb from which the new life will emerge.

In both sequences, the soul separates from the dying hermaphrodite and rises up to the realm of spirit, indicated by the clouds above. The spiritual dew, the essence of this first union, descends from the clouds, to re-animate the hermaphrodite and complete the first stage of the alchemical transformation.

"His soul rises up and is exalted to the heavens, that is, to the spirit ... And then the lantern with two lights, which is the water of life, will return to its origin, that is, to earth. And it becomes of low estate, is humbled and decays, and is joined to its beloved, the terrestrial sulphur [salt]."[5]

By virtue of her penetration by spirit, the feminine part of the soul gains her outline and definition, and becomes conscious of herself. She is reborn, now winged, to symbolise her newly realised spiritual nature, standing upon the crescent of the Moon, further emphasised by the appearance of the Moon tree on the left.

In the second sequence the king and queen are now winged, indicating the spiritual nature of their union. The solar disc descends into the vessel, and the wings are cast off as the spirit surrenders to the female forces of nature and of the earth. Once again, both die to their separateness, and once again the soul rises up towards the realm of Spirit before descending into a loving, conscious union with the now receptive male forces.

With the completion of the second stage, the hermaphrodite is reborn, this time clothed, ready to return to the world. The Sun tree is on the left, and behind the figure is a lion, another solar symbol. On the right, the pelican nourishes its young on the blood from its own breast.

The repeated separations and unions of the masculine and feminine aspects of the soul leads gradually to their equilibrium. Still differentiated, one from the other, they are no longer polarised by unconscious antipathy, no longer driven by lust, but united in love.

As ever, the spirit mercurius is the agent of the transformation, represented several times in both images of the reborn androgyne, as both a unity and a triplicity, as a serpent with one head and with three heads, symbolising the conscious interpenetration of spirit, soul and body.

A full blooded connection to life is now possible and we can taste the salt of life, often for the first time. As we discover the supreme value of our own unique subjectivity, we learn at last how to relate to our soul, to listen to its guidance and to heal its wounds.

The threefold nature of the soul

Ultimately, the influences of the outer planets are transformed by the *sublimatio, calcinatio* and *solutio* processes. These processes can only take place within the individual soul, through the conscious realisation and expression of insight and knowledge (spirit), wisdom and trust (body), love and compassion (soul). Uranus is no longer transcendant or dissociated from human values, but has become the spiritual source of revelation and knowledge. Pluto is no longer dark, hidden or destructive, but becomes the seat of primordial wisdom accessed through the body, instincts and nature. Neptune no longer dissolves or undermines the individual, but finds personal expression through unconditional love and service to the joys of the creative imagination.

Working together, in mutual support, the three parts of the soul – sulphur, mercury and salt – are at last brought into a state of harmony. "If, after purging them well, you join them together, they must by a natural process, result in a most pure substance."[6]

The third stage of the Coniunctio – The Sacred Marriage

"When you make the two into one, and when you make the inner like the outer and the outer like the inner, and the upper like the lower, and when you make male and female into a single one, so that the male will not be male nor the female be female ... then you will enter the Kingdom."[7]

The third stage of the *coniunctio* concerns the final symbolic union of the two formerly estranged aspects of the soul, the alchemical king and queen, heaven and earth, male and female.

"Learn from within thyself to know all that is in heaven and on earth, and especially that all was created for thy sake. Knowest thou not that heaven and the elements were formerly one, and were separated from one another by divine artifice, that they might bring forth thee and all things? ... Thou wilt never make from others the One which thou sleekest, except first there be made one thing of thyself."[8]

In the final transformation, the reconciled spirit/soul/body is united with the world in conscious wholeness. This stage is referred to as the *rubedo*, the redness, or blood, symbolised by the phoenix, the miraculous bird reborn from the ashes of the old, unconscious life. The awakening of the heart leads to a deeper compassion and commitment towards all living things, in the service of life itself.

In Figure 53, the earth is represented by the winged globe, to signify, perhaps, the incarnation of spirit in matter, the union of the masculine and feminine principles. The globe is quartered, as in the horoscope, to signify its existence in space and time, and further divided into, and united by the three and the four, the triangle of soul and the square of matter.

Mercurius, the instigator, mediator and conductor of the entire alchemical process is represented by the fire breathing dragon bestride the globe. The king and queen are reborn (rebis), now consciously united in the *coniunctio*, or indissoluble marriage of the above with the below. The king holds a compass, hermetic symbol of the heavens, representing the spiritual, intellectual and moral portion of the double nature of humanity. The queen holds a square, symbol of the productive earth, its material, sensual portion. As always, the entire drama is accompanied by the seven planets surrounding the central figure, and the whole image is enclosed within the cosmic egg.

Figure 53
Rebis – The cosmic egg

Endnotes

1. *The Emerald Tablet*, see Appendix 1.
2. Waite, E.A. *Hermetic Museum*, Vol 2, pp.142f.
3. Jung, C.G. (CW9) *Aion: Researches into the Phenomenology of the Self*.
4. See Appendix II – The Transits of Pluto.
5. Jung, C.G. (CW12) *Psychology and Alchemy*, para.292.
6. Waite, E.A., *Hermetic Museum*, Vol 2, pp.142f.
7. Gospel of Thomas, 22 [Discovered near Nag Hammadi, Egypt, in December 1945].
8. Dorn, G. Quoted by Jung in CW14, para 685.

Appendix I

The Emerald Tablet of Hermes

"According to legend, the original Emerald Tablet was found in the tomb of Hermes Trismegistus. The Emerald Tablet is a recipe for the Philosopher's Stone – the epitome of the alchemical opus. The alchemists treated it with unique veneration, engraving its statements on their laboratory walls and quoting it constantly in their works. It is also a summary of the individuation process."[1]

Truly, without deception, certain and most true. What is below is like that which is above, and what is above is like that which is below, to accomplish the miracles of the one thing.

And as all things proceeded from one, through mediation of the one, so all things come from this one thing through adaptation. Its father is the sun; its mother the moon; the wind has carried it in its belly; its nurse is the earth. This is the father of all, the completion of the whole world. Its strength is complete if it be turned into earth.

Separate the earth from the fire, the subtle from the dense, gently, and with great ingenuity. It ascends from the earth to heaven, and descends again to the earth, and receives the power of the above and the below. Thus you will have the glory of the whole world. Therefore all darkness will flee from you.

Here is the strong power of the whole strength; for it overcomes every subtle thing and penetrates every solid.

Thus the world has been created. From here will come the marvellous adaptations, whose manner this is.

So I am called Hermes Trismegistus, having the three parts of the philosophy of the whole world. What I have said about the operation of the sun in finished.

Endnote
1. Edinger, E.F. *The Mysterium Lectures*: A Journey through C.G. Jung's *Mysterium Coniunctionis*.

113

Appendix II
The Transits of Pluto

The Neptune/Pluto Cycle
We are all enclosed within the 492-year Neptune/Pluto cycle which began in the early 1890s. Identified as a cycle of compelling emotional force, inspiration and powerful collective ideals, almost all of us carry in our charts the fertile waxing sextile phase of this cycle, which continues for 82 years, from 1950 to 2032. The last waxing sextile period, between 1461 and 1540, saw the flowering of the Renaissance era and, once again, there are tremendous opportunities for individuals to capture and express the creative possibilities of this spirit of our times.

Transiting Pluto Conjunct Natal Neptune

Year of Birth	Pluto	Neptune	Pluto conjunct Natal Neptune	Age
1945	4° Leo	9° Lib	1975	30
1955	26° Leo	25 Lib	1981-82	26-27
1965	4° Vir	17° Sco	1990-91	25-26
1975	7° Lib	10° Sag	1999	24
1985	2° Sco	2° Cap	2009	24
1995	28° Sco	25° Cap	2020-21	25-26
2005	22° Sag	17° Aqu	2034-35	29-30

Transiting Pluto square Natal Pluto
Pluto's extremely elliptical orbit has had a profound effect on people born during the last half of the twentieth century. With Pluto moving relatively quickly round the birth chart, the calcinatio processes, with all their intensity and potential for change, have occurred more frequently than usual, and transiting Pluto has squared natal Pluto at a younger age.

Date of Birth	Natal Pluto	Pluto Waxing Square	Pluto Opposition
1940	Leo	45	85
1950	Leo	41	84
1960	Virgo	37	86
1970	Virgo	36	93
1980	Libra	38	106
1990	Scorpio	45	–

Bibliography

Atwood, M.A.	(1960) *Hermetic Philosophy and Alchemy*, 1850. Reprinted by The Julian Press, New York.
Baring, A.	(2013) *The Dream of the Cosmos: A Quest for the Soul*, Archive Publishing, Shaftsbury, Dorset.
	(2001) *C.G. Jung's Seven Sermons to the Dead*, Abzu Press, in conjunction with The Jupiter Trust, Oxford.
Baring, A. & Cashford, J.	(1991) *The Myth of the Goddess: Evolution of an Image*, Arkana, Penguin Books, London.
Burckhardt, T.	(2000) *Alchemy: Science of the Cosmos, Science of the Soul* (William Stoddart, translator), Fons Vitae, Louisville, KY. New Edition.
Campbell, J.	(1949) *The Hero with a Thousand Faces*, Paladin Books.
Campion, N.	(1994) *The Great Year: Astrology, Millenarianism and History in the Western Tradition*, Penguin, NY.
Cicero	(2008) *The Republic and The Laws*, Oxford World's Classics, OUP.
Edinger, E.F.	(1984) *The Creation of Consciousness: Jung's Myth for Modern Man*, Inner City Books, Toronto, Canada.
	(1985) *Anatomy of the Psyche, Alchemical Symbolism in Psychotherapy*, Open Court Publishing Company, La Salle, IL.
	(1994) *The Mystery of the Coniunctio: Alchemical Image of Individuation*, Inner City Books, Toronto, Canada.
	(1990) *Goethe's Faust: Notes for a Jungian Commentary*, Inner City Books, Toronto, Canada.
	(1995) *The Mysterium Lectures: A Journey through C.G. Jung's Mysterium Coniunctionis*, Inner City Books, Toronto, Canada.
Ebertin, R.	(2004) *The Combination of Stellar Influences*, American Federation of Astrologers, Tempe, AZ.

Eliade, M.   (1964) *Shamanism: Archaic Techniques of Ecstasy*,
                              English translation (1989) by Arkana, Penguin Books.

                              (1978) *The Forge and the Crucible*, Second Edition,
                              University of Chicago Press, English translation
                              (1962) by Rider & Company, London.

Gerber-Munch, I.   (2009) 'Goethe's Faust and the Myth of Modern
                              Man', *Psychological Perspectives: A Quarterly Journal
                              of Jungian Thought*, Volume 52, Issue 2.

Greene, L.   (1983) *The Outer Planets & Their Cycles: The
                              Astrology of the Collective*, CRCS Publications,
                              Nevada.

                              (1988) *Alchemical Symbolism in the Horoscope*,
                              in Dynamics of the Unconscious, Seminars in
                              Psychological Astrology, Vol 2, Samuel Weiser,
                              York Beach, ME.

Guthrie, K.S.   (1987), *Pythagorean Source Book and Library*, Phanes
                              Press, Grand Rapids, MI.

Hall, Manly P.   (1928) *The Secret Teachings of All Ages*, reprinted
                              in 2008 (University Edition) by the Philosophical
                              Research Society Inc., Los Angeles, CA.

Harpur, P.   (2003) *Daimonic Reality: A Field Guide to the
                              Otherworld*, Pine Winds Press, Enumclaw, WA.

Hartmann, F.   (1973) *Alchemy and Astrology, in Paracelsus: Life
                              and Prophecies*, Rudolf Steiner Publications, Forest
                              Row, E. Sussex.

Henderson, J.L. &   (2003) *Transformation of the Psyche, The Symbolic
Sherwood, D.N.   Alchemy of the Splendor Solis*, Routledge, London,
                              Taylor & Francis Group, London & New York.

Hillman, J.   (1972) *The Myth of Analysis*, North Western
                              University Press, Evanston, IL.

                              (1975) *Re-Visioning Psychology*, Harper Perennial,
                              New York.

                              (1980) *Facing the Gods*, Spring Publications, Inc.,
                              Dallas, TX.

                              (1981) 'Salt: A Chapter in Alchemical Psychology'
                              in *Images of the Untouched*, edited by J. Stroud and
                              G. Thomas, Spring Publications, Dallas, TX.

Bibliography

	(1989) *A Blue Fire: The Essential James Hillman*, Edited by Thomas Moore, Routledge, London.
Hillman, J. & Shamdasani, S.	(2013) *Lament of the Dead: Psychology After Jung's Red Book*, W.W. Norton & Company, NY.
Hollis, J.	(1998) *The Eden Project: In Search of the Magical Other*, Inner City Books, Toronto, Canada, p.17.
Johnson, R.	(1976) *She: Understanding Feminine Psychology*, Perennial Library, NY.
Jung, C.G.	(1969) *The Psychology of the Transference*, (3rd Edition), Princeton University Press, NJ.

(1973) *Memories, Dreams and Reflections*, ed. Aniela Jaffe, Pantheon, NY.

(1973) *Letters of C.G. Jung: Volume 1: 1906-1950*, eds. Gerhard Adler, Aniela Jaffé, Routledge, London.

(1976) *Letters, Volume 2: 1951-1961*, ed. Gerhard Adler, tr. Jeffrey Hulen, Princeton University Press. NJ.

(1976) *The Visions Seminars*, Zurich, Spring Publications, Washington, DC.

(1977) *C.G. Jung Speaking*, dd. W. McGuire & R.F.C. Hull, Princeton University Press, NJ.

(1989) *Neitzsche's Zarathustra*, Notes of the Seminars Given in 1934-39, Vol 2: 967-8, Routledge, London.

The Collected Works, ed by H. Read, M. Fordham, G. Adler.

(1970) CW Vol 8: *The Structure and Dynamics of the Psyche*.

(1959) CW Vol 9: *Aion – Researches into the Phenomenology of the Self*, Second Edition, Princeton, N.J. & Routledge and Kegan Paul Ltd., London.

(1970) CW Vol 11: *Psychology and Religion: West and East*.

(1968) CW Vol 12: *Psychology and Alchemy*, Second Edition, Routledge, London.

(1968) CW Vol 13: *Alchemical Studies*, translated from the German by R.F.C. Hull Jung, London and Henley, Routledge & Kegan Paul, London.

(1970) CW Vol 14: *Mysterium Coniunctionis: An Inquiry into the Separation and Synthesis of Psychic Opposites in Alchemy*, Second Edition, translated from the German by R.F.C. Hull, Princeton, N.J. & Routledge and Kegan Paul Ltd., London.

(2014) CW Vol 16: *The Practice of Psychotherapy*, Second Edition, translated by Gerhard Adler & R.F.C. Hull, Princeton University Press, NJ.

(1977) CW Vol 18: *The Symbolic Life: Miscellaneous Writings*, Routledge, London.

The Red Book

(1992) *The Gnostic Jung*: Including Seven Sermons to the Dead, Routledge, London.

(2009) *The Red Book: Liber Novus* ed. Sonu Shamdasani; trans by John Peck, Mark Kyburz & Sonu Shamdasani, W.W. Norton & Company, New York.

(2012) *The Red Book: A Reader's Edition* ed. Sonu Shamdasani; trans by John Peck, Mark Kyburz & Sonu Shamdasani, W.W. Norton & Company, New York.

(2013) *Lament of the Dead: Psychology After Jung's Red Book*, James Hillman & Sonu Shamdasani, W.W. Norton & Company, New York.

(2017) *Jung's Red Book for Our Time*, Volume 1, ed. Murray Stein & Thomas Arzt, Chiron Publications, Asheville, NC.

Kelly, E.   (1893) *The Alchemical Writings of Edward Kelly*, James Elliot, London.

Kingsley, P.   (1997) *Ancient Philosophy, Mystery, and Magic: Empedocles and Pythagorean Tradition*, Oxford University Press, New York.

(1999) *In the Dark Places of Wisdom* Golden Sufi Center, CA.

Bibliography

	(2003) Reality, Golden Sufi Center, CA.
	(2018) *Catafalque: Carl Jung and the End of Humanity* Catafalque Press, London.
Klossowski de Rola, S.	(1973) *Alchemy: The Secret Art*, Thames & Hudson, London.
Lowinsky, N.R.	(2009) 'The Devil and the Deep Blue Sea: Faust as Jung's Myth and Our Own, Psychological Perspectives', A *Quarterly Journal of Jungian Thought*, Volume 52
McClean, A.	A Commentary on the Rosarium Philosophorum: http://www.levity.com/alchemy/roscom.html
Moore, T.	(1982) *The Planets Within: The Astrological Psychology of Marsilio Ficino*, Lindisfarne Press edition 1990.
Needleman, J.	(1978) 'The Two Sciences of Medicine', in *Parabola Volume III, No.3, Inner Alchemy*, The Tamarack Press Inc. New York.
Neumann, E.	(1954) The Origins and History of Consciousness, Pantheon Books, New York.
Parabola	(1978) *Inner Alchemy*, Volume 3, Number 3, The Tamarack Press Inc. New York.
Perera, Silvia B.	(1989) *Descent to the Goddess: A Way of Initiation for Women*, Inner City Books, Toronto.
Plato	(2017) *Plato's Republic: The Myth of Er*, Akakia Publications, London.
Roberts, G.	(1995) *The Mirror of Alchemy: Alchemical Ideas and Images in Manuscripts and Books from Antiquity to the Seventeenth Century*, British Library Publishing Division
Rudhyar, D.	(1972) *The Pulse of Life: New Dynamics in Astrology*, Shambhala Publications, Boulder, CO.
	(1987) *The Astrological Houses: The Spectrum of Individual Experience*, CRCS Publications, Nevada.
Schwartz-Salant, N. (ed)	(1995) C.G. Jung: Jung on Alchemy, Routledge, London.

Somé, M.

(1999) *The Healing Wisdom of Africa*, Jeremy P. Tarcher, (Penguin) New York.

Somers, B.

(2004) *The Fires of Alchemy: A Transpersonal Viewpoint*, Archive Publishing, Shaftsbury, Dorset.

Stein, M.

(2014) *In Midlife: A Jungian Perspective*, Chiron Publications, Asheville, NC.

Stern, K.

(1965) *The Flight from Woman*, reprinted in 1985 by Paragon House Publishers, New York, NY

Von Franz, M-L.

(1975) *C.G. Jung: His Myth in Our Time*, G.P. Putnam & Sons, New York, for the C.G. Jung Foundation for Analytical Psychology.

(1980) *Alchemy: An Introduction to the Symbolism and the Psychology*, Inner City Books, Toronto, Canada.

(2000) *Aurora Consurgens*, Inner City Books; New Edition

Waite, A.E.

(1888) 'Artefius: Clavis majoris sapientiae', in *Lives of the Alchemystical Philosophers*, J. Elliot, London

(1967) *The Hermetic and Alchemical Writings of Paracelsus*, University Books, New Hyde Park, NY.

(1991) *The Hermetic Museum*, Vol 2, Samuel Weiser, Inc York Beach, ME.

Wehr, G.

(1986) *The Mystical Marriage: Symbol and Meaning of the Human Experience*, Crucible, Thorsons Publishing Group Northamptonshire,

Whitmont, E.C.

(1982) *Return of the Goddess*, Routledge & Kegan Paul Ltd, London; Penguin Arkana, London edition, 1987.

(1991) *Psyche and Substance: Essays on Homoeopathy in the Light of Jungian Psychology*, North Atlantic Books, Berkeley, CA.

(1993) *The Alchemy of Healing: Psyche and Soma*, North Atlantic Books.

Index

About the Author

Clare Martin is an integrative psychotherapist and has been a professional astrologer, teacher and lecturer for over thirty years. Former President of the Faculty of Astrological Studies (www.astrology. org.uk), Clare presided over the Faculty's annual Summer Schools in Oxford for nine years, attended by students, teachers and lecturers from all over the world. In 2009 she was awarded the Faculty's Fellowship for her exceptional service to astrological education. Clare was also a regular lecturer and supervisor of Diploma students at the Centre for Psychological Astrology (www.cpalondon.com).

Clare is the author of *Mapping the Psyche*, published by The Wessex Astrologer, a three volume Introduction to Psychological Astrology based on the beginners' course she taught at the CPA. She is now living in Dorset, where she continues her astrological consultancy work and is a tutor for the Mercury Internet School of Psychological Astrology (www.mercuryinternetschool.com).

Website: www.claremartin.net

Lightning Source UK Ltd.
Milton Keynes UK
UKHW021827110820
368070UK00004B/159